AGEING IN NORTH EAST INDIA

Arunachal Pradesh Perspectives

AGEING IN NORTH EAST INDIA

Arunachal Pradesh Perspectives

Edited by

DR. R.M. PANT

AKANSHA PUBLISHING HOUSE
NEW DELHI-110002 (INDIA)

AKANSHA PUBLISHING HOUSE
4649-B/21, Ansari Road
Darya Ganj, New Delhi - 110 002
Ph.: 23263193 / 9811582579 / 09435116718
Telefax: 011-23263193
Email: ektabooks@yahoo.com

Ageing in North East India: Arunachal Pradesh Perspectives

First Published 2008

Reprint 2026

ISBN 978–81–8370–139-6

PRINTED IN INDIA

Published by M.P. Misra for Akansha Publishing House, New Delhi and Printed at Mehra Offset, Delhi.

Dedicated to

My Father

Late Dr. DAMODAR PANT,

who served the society with indefatigable dedication and lived with flamboyance till his last breath.

CONTENTS

FOREWORD

In the recent years, much literature on North-East India has been published by the scholars of this region on various issues related to the people and the region as a whole. However, the issues related to ageing, the elderly persons of this region are not properly addressed so far. Although every 1st October is being observed as the international day for the elderly, yet the magnitude of the problems of the elderly persons in North-East India is not properly addressed neither in the myriad seminars organized by the various academic bodies and the NGO's nor their problems and aspirations are documented.

Considering the lacunae in this field, the Indian Council of Social Science Research, North Eastern Regional Centre (ICSSR-NERC), Shillong took the initiative to bridge the gap by organizing a day long seminar on the magnitude of the problems of the elderly persons in North-East during 2006-2007. This book has its origin in one of the seminars organized by the Department of Humanities and Social Sciences, North Eastern Regional Institute of Science and Technology (NERIST), Itanagar, Arunachal Pradesh on November 18, 2006. Dr R M Pant and his colleagues in the department took the keen interest in the seminar not only in organizing it but also compiling and revising the papers presented in the seminar in the present book format.

The papers carefully put together for this volume by R M Pant raise some of the vital questions related to the elderly persons in the State of Arunachal Pradesh and will, I am sure, prove to be essential reading for anyone interested in the field of ageing.

C. J. Thomas
Acting Director

ICSSR-NERC
Shillong

PREFACE

The rising population of aged and elderly is an emerging concern for social demographers as well as for policy-makers. This shift in the population structure is taking place mainly due to longer life expectancies and falling birth rate. Even among the aged, the problem of old women, divorced, single and widowed population is different from those of aged males. A very high rate of rural-urban migration also creates psychological, social and economic problems for the elderly.

Among the indigenous people, who are experiencing very rapid transition from their simple community life in rural and many a times inhospitable areas, to a life in rapidly growing towns and over burdened cities, the aged and elderly are facing severe problems of poverty, ill health, isolation and complete neglect. On the other hand, when the aged are taken along to urban areas, by the migrating younger relatives, it creates another set of problems. The health care system is quite inadequate and there is hardly any specialized agency focusing on the problems of aged and elderly people in fast emerging urban centers. The problem becomes more serious in the absence of any programmes available to train people for taking care of aged. Thus the responsibility of caring aged remains with the traditional institution of family and kinship network, which are also getting transformed due to several forces of change.

The gradual marginalization of the elderly in the decision making process in an average family and the breakdown of the family as a traditional social unit that took care of elderly in the transitional society. It is also important to recognize that with rising number of old persons and their changing socio-economic and physical context, the proportion of the destitute may also be rising. This is more prevalent among the indigenous people in the different parts of the country.

Arunachal, the land of dawn-lit sun is experiencing changes at all the fronts in an unprecedented pace and these rapid changes are taking its toll in terms of socio-economic and psychological anxieties among its population. Elderly and aged people are most vulnerable to these changing realities.

Need of the hour is to understand the problems of aged and elderly people in Arunachal Pradesh in their right perspective as this tribal state offers a diverse cultural canvas. Each tribe has its own indigenous social systems, which too stand exposed to the wind of change.

To probe in to this growing problem a seminar on the topic 'The problem of aged and elderly in indigenous communities of North East India with special reference to Arunachal Pradesh' was conceptualized. With generous financial support from the Indian Council of Social Science Research, North Eastern Regional Centre (ICSSR-NERC), Shillong and encouragement from Dr

C.J Thomas, Director, ICSSR-NERC, this seminar was conducted on November 18, 2006. Researchers, academicians, social workers and people from diverse backgrounds participated in this seminar actively and the highlight of this event was the participation of the elderly people themselves.

Following papers were presented in the seminar:

1. 'Problem of Aged and Elderly with reference to Arunachal Pradesh', P Lingfa, Senior Lecturer, Department of Mechanical Engineering, NERIST, Nirjuli.
2. 'Problems of the Aged in Arunachal Pradesh: Reflections', Dr Tado Karlo, Chairman, (NIHRO), Itanagar, Arunachal Pradesh.
3. 'Globalization and the Future of Aging in an Indigenous Society', Pratul Joshi, Programme Executive, AIR, Itanagar.
4. 'The Problem of Aged and Elderly in Indigenous Communities of Arunachal Pradesh, North East India', Dr. S J Neethirajan, Senior Lecturer and Mrs D S Sworna Latha, (MBA 1st year student), Department of Humanities and Social Sciences, NERIST, Nirjuli.
5. 'A Socio-Economic Study on Aged Persons in Arunachal Pradesh', Dr B D Nayak, Senior Lecturer, Department of Humanities and Social Sciences, NERIST, Nirjuli and Dr (Mrs.) Shipra Sarkar, Freelance Researcher, Nirjuli, Arunachal Pradesh.

6. 'Ageing and Psycho-social Development', Dr P Parida, Assistant Professor, Department of Humanities and Social Sciences, NERIST, Nirjuli.
7. 'Problems of Aged and Elderly Indigenous Communities of North East India with a special reference to Arunachal Pradesh' Pradeep Kumar, Editor, *Arunachal Times*, Itanagar.
8. 'Ageing Population in Arunachal Pradesh – A Comparative Study', Dr R P Bhattacharjee, Secretary, APISSR, Itanagar.
9. 'Globalization, the Traditional *Arunachalee* Identity and the Psycho-social Gap of the Aged and the Elderly', Raju Barthakur.
10. 'Welfare Schemes for the Aged: Scenario in Arunachal Pradesh', R P Bhattacharjee and R M Pant.

Some other prominent scholars of the state i.e. Professor T Mibang, Pro Vice-Chancellor, Rajiv Gandhi University, Arunachal Pradesh, Professor Pura Tado, Department of Political Science, Rajiv Gandhi University, Arunachal Pradesh also enlightened the audience with their presentations on the issues related to the problem of aged people in Arunachal Pradesh. Some elderly persons, invited to share their views with the researchers and the audience, were felicitated.

Out of the day long seminar that provided some useful insights to the problem of aged population of Arunachal Pradesh, some papers are being presented in this book with the hope that this will provide a starting point in finding solutions to the problems that today's elderly population is facing, and that today's young generation shall also be facing tomorrow.

At the end, I take this opportunity to express my deep sense of indebtedness to the Indian Council of Social Sciences Research–North Eastern Center, Shillong for their generous financial support for carrying out this work. I would like to acknowledge the contribution of Dr C. J. Thomas who not only conceptualized the idea but also motivated me for this noble work. I acknowledge the contribution of my friends Dr. Ashish Pandey, (IIT, Roorkee) and Dr. S.K.Tapaswi, (MDI, Gurgaon), who helped me in organizing this seminar, which paved the way for this publication. Mr Angad Barman, my departmental colleague also deserves appreciation for his contribution in sprucing up the designing aspects of this volume.

I also acknowledge the support I received from my family members, friends and colleagues, without which this work would not have been possible. I sincerely hope that this collective effort will serve the purpose for which we all worked.

R.M. Pant

NERIST, Nirjuli

LIST OF CONTRIBUTORS

Barthakur, Raju, Lecturer, Department of Humanities & Social Sciences, North Eastern Regional Institute of Science & Technology, Nirjuli, Arunachal Pradesh

Bhattacharjee, R P, Secretary, APISSR, Itanagar, Arunachal Pradesh

Joshi, Pratul, Programme Executive, All India Radio, Itanagar

Karlo,Tado, Chairman, NEFA Indigenous Human Rights Organization, (NIHRO), Itanagar, Arunachal Pradesh.

Kumar, Pradeep, Editor, *The Arunachal Times*, Itanagar, Arunachal Pradesh.

Nayak B D, Department of Humanities & Social Sciences, North Eastern Regional Institute of Science & Technology,Nirjuli, Arunachal Pradesh

Neethirajan S J, Senior Lecturer, Department of Humanities & Social Sciences, North Eastern Regional Institute of Science & Technology, Nirjuli, Arunachal Pradesh

Pant, R M, Head, Department of Humanities & Social Sciences, North Eastern Regional Institute of Science & Technology, Nirjuli, Arunachal Pradesh.

Parida, P, Assistant Professor, Department of Humanities & Social Sciences, North Eastern Regional Institute of Science & Technology, Nirjuli, Arunachal Pradesh.

Prasanna Kumar, G V, Lecturer, Agricultural Engineering Department, North Eastern Regional Institute of Science & Technology, Nirjuli, Arunachal Pradesh

Sarkar, Shipra, Freelance Researcher

Sworna Latha D S, MBA Student, Department of Humanities & Social Sciences, North Eastern Regional Institute of Science & Technology, Nirjuli, Arunachal Pradesh

1

In Search of Solutions: Aged and Elderly in Arunachal Pradesh

—R.M. Pant

The quiet land that lived in isolation for long years broke its silence suddenly after Independence. Especially past two decades were quite prominent in the development of Arunachal. From a sleeping, stagnant and subsistence economy to a march towards rapidly moving economic activities to keep pace with rest of the world, saw Arunachal emerging out of its hibernation in last two decades. This rapid economic change brought economic prosperity and opened new vistas but changed the age-old socio-economic scenario in the state. As it is rightly said that, 'In a changing environment, all those who fail to change, face entropy'. In every society, there are few sections in the society who do not respond to changes with the same pace fall victim to changing demands and become vulnerable to face entropy. Elderly people fall in that category, as they find it difficult to come out of the fetters of traditional living that have had lived with for years. They have spent long years in developing expertise in some area, they have lived in their own way and suddenly when the 'rules of the game' change, they find it difficult to adjust to these changes and left to sufferings. Elderly population in Arunachal seems to be standing at the crossroads, looking for solutions for this unprecedented phenomenon.

Elderly population in the 21st Century continue to live primitive life

20th and 21st century ushered human civilization to new heights with so many inventions and innovations. Advancement in healthcare sector has improved longevity. Long life expectancy and falling birth rate are welcome changes in Indian condition, but they are at the same time bringing in some complications. Lesser active manpower and more mouths to feed is an agony for bread earners; and it can be a psychological nightmare for the elders. Elderly population is showing rising trends in India. In the year 1996, the share of elderly population was only 6.7% of the total population of India, which rose to 9% in the year 2006 and according to an estimate, it will rise to 21.2% by 2050.

Scenario is equally alarming in Arunachal Pradesh. The Table 1 suggests the age-wise composition of the population in Arunachal in the year 1991.

Table-1
Age wise composition of population in Arunachal in the year 1991

Age Group	*Total population*
0-14	3,45,933
15-29	2,32146
30-49	1,95759
50 and above	85,683
Total	8,59,521

Source: Census 1991

As per the 2001 census, Arunachal's population has gone up to 10,97,968 and a conservative estimate suggests addition of another 2,00,000 persons in the age group of 50 plus population, that makes the share of elderly population a one fourth of the total population in the state. Facilities to take care of their health and hygiene (Table-2) remain almost static and inadequate, making the plight of elderly miserable. This situation is undoubtedly sending alarming signals for the planners to wake up.

Table-2
Total number of medical (allopathic) institutions in Arunachal Pradesh

General Hospitals (Govt)	General Hospital (NGO)	District Hospitals
02	01	12

Source: Directorate of Health Services.

In addition to the above, 17 family welfare clinics are also operational in Arunachal, albeit with extremely poor facilities. Three Ayurvedic hospitals (2 government and one private) are also serving the state with minimum facilities. All these health institutions together fail to meet the total demand for health facilities and remain inadequate and primitive.

High Migration rate and enhanced sufferings for elderly

With the concentration of opportunities in urban areas, more and more youth are attracted to the glamour of urban life. Be it education or employment, these opportunities exist only in urban Arunachal. Rural Arunachal continue to languish and this is causing mass exodus from rural areas to urban centers. From the year 1991-2001, Aruchal Pradesh has witnessed a population growth at the rate 26.85 %(Table 3), which is higher than the national average of 21.34 Urban centers like Itanagar, Bomdi-la, Changlang etc. have seen a sharp population rise. Papum Pare district (Capital complex of Arunachal Pradesh falls in this district) experienced maximum decadal growth in the state with a rise in population with 67.31% figure. One of the main reasons for this growth is the entry of immigrants from different parts of the state. With the exodus of working population from rural areas, elderly and women are left to face the hardships in the villages with virtually no facilities. This growing trend is creating psychological, social and economic problems for elderly. All those who accompany the young ones to urban centers, find it difficult to adjust to their new surroundings and soon begin to feel nostalgic for their native places.

Rapid transition from simple community life in rural areas to the life of overburdened and fast life of cities is causing problems in social setup and affecting the social fabric of Arunachalees. Urban life has brought about a significant shift in decision-making process in favour of the younger generation that is more educated and has more exposure. Aloofness, poverty, ill health and neglect are some other factors that are gripping elderly in Arunachal.

Table-3
Population Growth Trends

Population	Decadal Growth rate %	Population density	Literacy rate 2001	Percentage of Urban population
10,97,968	26.85	13	54.74	20.41

Source: Statistical Abstract of Arunachal Pradesh, 2003.

Few relevant questions

Humans are being treated as resources, just like money, machine and any other material resource in this material world. In this material order where productivity dictates human behavior, as long as people are contributing in production, they are resources and valued. Once they cease to do that, they become liabilities. Is it proper to treat humans as resource? Is 'elderly' population an effete resource? Is it proper to view 'social phenomenon' from economics or market angles? Is tangible output the only parameter to evaluate a person's worth? These questions echo in today's Arunachal that need to be answered on ethical grounds.

Wonderful schemes that never saw the light of the day

Fast changing complexion of Arunachal's population is causing concern in the minds of leaders, policy makers and social workers, and often these concerns are expressed. However, when it comes to implementing schemes to tackle these problems, hardly any tangible interventions are initiated from the government as well as by the NGO sector. Some populist schemes mentioned below were initiated for senior citizens in the state:

1. *Old age pension scheme*: State sector scheme: Rs 150 per month to people between 60-65 years of age.
2. *National old age pension scheme*: Rs 75 P.M. to people above 65 years. State government to pay Rs 75 to make the total benefit Rs 150 per month.
3. *Scheme of assistance for voluntary organizations* to encourage them to provide old age homes, day care centers and non-institutional services for the aged are also launched. Organizations eligible for assistance are voluntary organizations, Panchayati raj institutions, Municipal bodies and charitable trusts. 95% assistance is provided from government while 5 % fund has to be arranged by the organization. These schemes are aimed at providing the following:

- Mobile Medicare services for the aged for consultation and treatment
- Day care centers to supplement activities of families in looking after the need of aged.
- At least 50 persons in one center.
- Old age homes–residential units for at least 25 aged persons.

These seemingly wonderful schemes failed due to lack of will and skill on the part of the government and remained buried in official files. Virtually no effect of these schemes is seen in Arunachal. No proper mechanism exists to identify the beneficiary groups. Bureaucracy fails to provide any solution to this socio-economic problem of the elderly population. What is required is a philanthropic solution with a participative approach from the different stakeholders in the society.

Where does the solution lie?

To optimists, there is no problem, which does not have a solution. Problem of aged and elderly is a new phenomenon in Arunachal Pradesh, as this state is going through a transition phase. Rapid development has shaken some traditional systems and society is finding it difficult to overcome the inertia. However, this problem needs to be tackled and solutions are to be found sooner than later. Following interventions from government as well non-government sector provide the solution to the problem of elderly population:

1. Old age homes and better healthcare facilities are to be established with Government and NGO participation. Industrial houses should also be encouraged to discharge their social responsibilities. Jamshedpur (Tatanagar) model can be emulated to improve the plight of elderly and needy population of Arunachal Pradesh.

2. New and innovative social security schemes are needed in Arunachal. Arunachal Pradesh can boast of having some premier academic institutions in the state and also it has a galaxy of brilliant officers and intellectuals in its cadre. Brainstorming sessions can provide some viable solutions to the problems of elderly people with affordable investment. What is required is to lead the thinking in the right direction.

3. Arunachal being the biggest state of the North East Region of India (area-wise) suffers from the problem of lack of infrastructure. Given its limited resources, it may not be possible immediately to set up necessary infrastructural support in the areas of health, public distribution systems (PDS) etc. However, to some extent, this problem can be eased with mobile health centers and PDS.

4. As a part of long term strategy, PURA, a much talked about visionary scheme of our President, Dr A P J Abdul Kalam, provides solution to this problem. PURA or Providing Urban facilities in Rural Areas will not only check migration from rural areas and but will also check sagging value system in the society. This will also help strengthen our traditional family system that has sustained since time immemorial.

Indian value system rightly prescribes that, 'In a society, where elders are respected, people are blessed with all four qualities i.e. Longevity, Knowledge, Fame and Power'.

REFERENCES

1. *Staistical Abstract of Arunachal Pradesh*, 2003
2. *Arunachal Pradesh at a Glance*, 2003
3. *Manusmriti.*

2

Problems of Aged and Elderly Indigenous Communities of North East India with a Special Reference to Arunachal Pradesh

—Pradeep Kumar

Ageing is a natural biological phenomenon for every living human being. 'Every mortal being has to perish' is a gospel truth. But most of us shiver at the very feeling of becoming old. For, the last phase of life has lot of unending problems-social, physical, mental, health and so on and so forth.

John Buchan once said, "As we age, the mystery of Time more and more dominates the mind. We live less in the present, which no longer has the solidity that it had in youth; less in the future, for the future every day narrows its span. The abiding things lie in the past."

Notwithstanding these problems, India being a democratic society gives the status of head of the family to the old and aged ones and their advices and wishes are honoured. They are cared for not neglected unlike

Communist China, where 'no work, no food' or 'eat according to your capacity' principle governs the society.

The old and aged people being the major component of the society, Article 41 of the Indian constitution under the Direct Principles of State Policy has made old age welfare policy mandatory. Besides grant of old age pension by some state governments, including Arunachal Pradesh, various facilities to the senior citizens above the age of 60 are granted as per the central government rules. Though these welfare measures ethically can't be converted to a banker's cheque payable when able in state's policy. So there is a conviction to protect the 'wisdom' as it is the need of 21st century. The reason being 'Gandhism' is still relevant in 21st century nuclear holocaust. With the fast changing social setup, particularly nucleus family pattern, effect of modernization, craze for urbanization and the compulsion of the offsprings to stay away from homes in search of livelihood, the problems of the old parents left alone at homes to fend for themselves are aggravating day by day. Though there are old age homes run by voluntary organizations in various parts of the country to take care of this segment of the population, all are not lucky to reach such centers.

These are insufficiently sufficient only in case of urban populace. Remember old age is not either a rural or urban problem but a social reality in every structure.

If one considers the North East India, particularly Arunachal Pradesh, the problem is not acute because of community or clan living system. Those in ripe age are becoming the victim of alienation setting in the process, which would show up its ugly head in not so distant future. Cases are not noticed but ignored intentionally by policy-makers.

Early and child marriage are the greatest factors to ageing process in NE India, particularly in Arunachal where the life expectancy is 54 years as the people get older at an early age. Lack of adequate medical care in remote and far-flung areas, food habits and unhygienic living conditions expedite the process further in this part of the country. However, culture is the strongest force in the region, where every one is inter-woven to the society with a specific assigned responsibility.

What this segment of population need at this stage are love, compassion, understanding and empathy and lack of it would put them to a state of misery when every moment they would live a miserable life waiting for death to embrace them. The near and dear ones despite their old age would change their outlook towards life if their state of misery is changed to a state of felicity.

Who would solve this problem? — is a million dollar question with the present generation becoming too self-centric. The society at large and the state governments in particular should evolve a pragmatic approach towards channelizing the wisdom and capability of the old and aged ones to benefit the society while making the last part of their life meaningful and blissful.

I would like to advocate a multi-pronged strategy involving various sections of the society to overcome such societal problem.

1) **Rehabilitation:** Rehabilitation should begin at home, for Southey says: **"There is a magic in that word, home; it is a mystic circle that surrounds comforts and virtues never known beyond its hallowed limits".** Otherwise, the issue should be tackled at community level so that no aged person goes uncared for.

2) **Productive employment:** North East, particularly this Himalayan state is known for its rich handicrafts and handlooms, art and architect. The experienced aged ones could be engaged in training members of the community in their respective field of expertise, while the community takes their care. They would be given productive employment while getting rehabilitated in the process.

3) **Cultural archive:** The rich cultures, folk lores and folk songs of Arunachal Pradesh passed from generation to generation orally are yet to be documented. The art and culture department could consider setting up a cultural archive and utilize the wisdom and knowledge of the aged and old ones, the real custodians of art and culture, to preserve the cultural ethos before their extinction.

4) **Indigenous knowledge:** When I was serving in Donyi-Polo Vidya Bhawan, Itanagar in 80's, state Chief Minister and chairman of the vidyalaya, Shree Gegong Apang arrived once with an aged local *Vaidyaraj* (doctor), who knew only local

dialects. Perhaps, he was a blessed soul for he had the capacity to have a glimpse of a person and describe all his ailments without even touching him/her with the CM interpreting his version. Such unique knowledge is rarest and should be documented or passed on to the next generation to benefit the entire humanity.

There are local persons highly knowledgeable in use of medicinal herbs and plants available aplenty in the state for treating various chronic ailments. If documented such wisdom gained through years of personal experience could be of immense use for the entire human kind.

The requirements of the indigenous aged and old people need an empathetic consideration much above the official paraphernalia. The famous English poet Shakespeare in his famous novel *'Much Ado About Nothing'* has described vividly about the old age wisdom. Dante's classic *'Divine Comedy'* has, however, added weightage to the Shakespearean philosophy that such wisdom is always considered an assent in strengthening the social fabric.

If at all Arunachal is to reap the benefits of LPG (liberalization, privatization, globalization), the protection of the 'old age' to ensure 'age old' to be the moving mechanisms. Take for example the traditional indigenous segment of healing is being discussed with priority by our state policy makers to bring it into intellectual property right (IPR). The state chief minister has got it approved for the state. The question comes—can we execute without this 'old age wisdom'?

Can the urbanized young show the initiative to full fill the mission? The answer is a big paradox. So better late than never!

Why not put our hands and heads together to utilize the old men's wisdom while paving a smooth passage for their last journey? For, I and most of you will enter the same phase tomorrow, which was one of the four impacting scenes that had turned Prince Suddhodana to Lord Buddha. I am not a prince neither I would be a saint, but I can not escape old age.

3

Ageing and Psycho-Social Development

—P. Parida

[It describes a framework for understanding how age-related changes in the development process affect cognitive abilities, personality, values, and self-concept. People age in different ways depending on a large variety of factors, including their gender, ethnic and cultural backgrounds, climate, geographical location, family size, life skills, experience, etc. Further it indicates that the characterization of adult ageing as a process of decline is incomplete. In the intellectual domain, while there is decline in fluid intellectual abilities, at the same time there is increase in crystallized intellectual abilities. In the personality domain, some personality traits decline (e.g. openness to experience) while other traits show an increase (conscientiousness). In the domain of work motivation, there is no change in middle and later years as shown in young adulthood. Therefore, it is important to acknowledge that chronological age is not a precise marker for the changes that accompany ageing. There are dramatic variations in health status ('health' refers to physical, mental, and social well-being as expressed in the WHO definition of health), participation and levels of independence among older people of the same age. Decision-makers need to take this into account when designing policies and programs

> for their 'older' population. Enacting broad social policies based on chronological age alone can be discriminatory and counterproductive to well-being in older age].

Ageing is defined as the process of progressive change in the biological, psychological, and social structure of individuals. For statistical purposes, 'the aged' are commonly placed into specific age groups, for example, those aged 60 years and above, depending on cultural, and personal perceptions. However, ageing is a life-long process, which begins before we are born and continues throughout life. We are all ageing–everyday of our life. Every one of us started to age before we were born and we continue to do so throughout entire life. Ageing is a natural process and should be welcomed, because the alternative would be premature death. But the problem is older people are often viewed as homogenous group, who no longer contribute to their families and societies, and may even be a burden.

Life expectancy has risen sharply this century, and is expected to continue to rise, in virtually all populations throughout the world. The number of people reaching old age is therefore increasing. There are currently 600 million people in the world who are aged 60 years or older. This figure is expected to rise to 1.2 billion in 2025 and 70% will be in developing countries. By 2050 there will be 2 billion with 80 percent of them living in developing countries and one out of every five persons will be above 60. Remarkably, in very old age women will outnumber men in the ratio of 2:1.

In India, 90% of older persons are having no social security at the age of 60. Thirty percent of older persons live below the poverty line and another 33% just marginally over it. Eighty percent live in rural areas and 73% are illiterate, and can only be engaged in physical labour. Fiftyfive percent of women over 60 are widows, many of them with no support whatsoever. There are nearly 200,000 centenarians in India.

Sharp increases of life expectancy have been accompanied by substantial falls in fertility all over the world, mainly due to modern contraceptive methods. In India, for example, total fertility rates (that is the total number of children a woman is expected to borne) have decreased from 5.9 in 1970 to 3.1 in 1998. In Brazil, fertility rates dropped from 5.1 in 1970 to 2.2 in 1998. This decline is even more pronounced in China, where fertility rates fell from 5.5 in 1970 to the current 1.8 which is below the 2.1 replacement level.

This trend, by which more people live to reach older age, while fewer children are born, is referred to as "population ageing". It has been particularly rapid in developing countries. It is estimated that by 2025, 120 countries will reach total fertility rates below replacement level, substantial increase compared to 1975, when just 22 countries had a total fertility rate below or equal to the replacement level, whereas the current figure is 70.

As more people reach a "ripe old age", they enter a period in their lives when they are at higher risks of developing chronic diseases, which in turn may result in disability. It is projected that in many countries with fertility rates below replacement level, the proportion of older people is expected to exceed the proportion of the very young (aged up to 19 years) by 2050. In all countries and in developing countries in particular, measures to help older people remain healthy and active are a necessity, not a luxury.

Active Ageing

Active aging is the process of optimizing opportunities for health, participation and security in order to enhance quality of life as people age. Among the many dimensions of "the situation of older persons", two are emerging to pre-eminence- active aging and care giving strategies. The term "active aging" or "productive aging" are currently used in two ways: first, to describe, and thereby support, the importance of the many socially and economic productive roles open to aging individuals in developing countries and secondly, as an attempt to reverse the phenomenon in developed countries whereby retirement from the formal economic sector automatically negates the formal acknowledgement of the unpaid productive roles of many older persons.

Health is vital to maintain wellbeing and quality of life in older age, and is essential if older citizens are to continue making contributions to society. The vast majority of old people enjoy sound health, lead very active and fulfilling lives, and can muster intellectual, emotional, and social reserves often unavailable to younger people.

People age in unique ways, depending on a large variety of factors, including their gender, ethnic and cultural backgrounds, and whether they live in industrialized or developing countries, in urban or social settings. Climate, geographical location, family size, life skills, and experience are all factors that make people less and less alike as they advance in age.

Many studies have shown that there are wide variations in patterns of disease in people from different ethnic and cultural communities which largely unexplained.

Promoting Active Ageing

Individual development through the different stages of the life cycle requires both individual initiative and enabling environment. Individual development can be viewed as a process of interaction between the individual and society which can be mutually beneficial. At the individual level, this implies concerted effort to combine individual independence with contributory/ participatory behavior, while striving towards self-development through life-long education, upgrading of skills and healthy life styles. Society needs to accord equal importance to the challenges of each stage of the life cycle.

When the majority of individuals can pursue life-long individual development, an ageing population can reach maturity not only in terms of demography, but also of intellect and emotion. This would help ensure, among other things, the years added to life could be infused with new sense of purpose and liveliness appreciated at both individual and collective level.

Age and Gender

Women live longer than men. The oldest old, in most

part of the world, are predominantly women. Although women live longer than men, they tend to experience disabling diseases as they grow older compared with men of the same age. There is also a wide variation in the perceived need for certain functional abilities among older people. In some societies, for example, fetching water and firewood are tasks traditionally carried out by women. Maintaining maximum functional capacity is as important for older people as freedom from diseases.

Age and Emotion

Researchers have focused broadly on three aspects: experience, expressivity, and control. Gross et al. (1977) suggest that age-related declines in emotion expressivity may be limited to negative emotions and that ageing is associated with improvement in emotion regulation, particularly in terms of the use of cognitive emotion regulation strategies. It has been found by Blanchard-Fields and Irwin (1988) that older adults make more frequent use of emotional control strategies than younger adults.

Age and Self-concept

It has been found that most individuals are sensitive to changes in their abilities with increasing age and typically seek to act in ways that serve to protect their overreaching self-concept. That is, with the transition from young adulthood into middle age and beyond, individuals see themselves as possessing lower abilities. Protecting self-concepts seem to be one of the leading determinants of middle aged and older adults' avoidance of some kinds of career development activities.

Age and Values

Ryff and Baltes (1976) suggest that as individuals move from middle to old age, they tend to show a diminution of "instrumental" values (such as financial security) but an increased orientation toward "terminal" values (such as a desire for world peace).

Age and Personality

It has been observed that there are mean, age-related changes in trait levels across the life span (Jones and Meredith, 1996). Extroversion, neuroticism, and openness to experience all show mean declines with age so that older adults can be expected, on average, to be less active, less anxious, and less open to new experiences than younger adults. In contrast, increase in mean levels of conscientiousness and agreeableness, over the life span; have been observed in several studies. Warr, Miles, and Platts (2001) have shown significant age differences in conscientiousness, with older adults more conscientious but less sociable, out going, change oriented, and career-motivated than younger adults.

Age and Work Motivation

There is neither theoretical justification nor empirical evidence to support the notion of an inevitable and universal decline in work motivation with age. Kanfer and Ackerman (2004) suggest that work motivation in middle and later years follows the same basic principles as work motivation in young adulthood.

Age and Cognitive Activities

The findings indicate a gradual decline in cognitive

activities over the life span, particularly those associated with fluid intelligence (working memory, abstract reasoning, attention, and processing of novel information). In contrast to fluid intelligence, measures of crystallized intelligence (knowledge, skills, extend of vocabulary, verbal comprehension) show increasing levels of performance well into middle age and beyond.

Culture and Ageing

Culture which surrounds all individuals and population shapes the way in which people age because it influences all of the other determinants of active ageing. When societies are more likely to attribute symptoms of disease to the ageing process, they are less likely to provide prevention, early detection, and appropriate treatment services. Social perceptions of the value and benefits of old age vary in different countries. In many African and Asian countries, words which describe older people characterize them as 'someone with knowledge'. However, in some cultures these traditional values are in danger of being eroded. It is important to recognize that ageing is not an affliction but a great opportunity to make use of resources acquired over the life course, and that older people can be a tremendous asset to families and community.

Conclusion

Although the individual may not have control over early life experiences and other factors such as poverty or low education, actions (works for older persons, pension) taken during the remaining life course greatly affect the health in later life. For older people living in poverty and social isolation have adverse effects on health. Playing a part in family life, and being a member of a community or religious organization have beneficial effects on health, improve a person's self-worth and enable older people to make a greater contribution to society.

In addition, policy decisions to encourage healthy, active ageing must include the creation of supportive social and environmental conditions throughout life. Macro-level decisions can also help to ensure that the total living environment supports multi-generational exchanges, active ageing in place, and a culture of caring from which all benefit, for example, establishing programs to support self-help and family care-giving, as well as by encouraging a continuum of housing arrangements from 'granny flats' to community integrated long-term care facilities.

In period of demographic and socio-economic transitions, reference to the United Nations' Principles for Older Persons can help to ensure that macro-level policies take into account the independence, participation, care, self-fulfillment, and dignity of older persons.

In short, population ageing is not a crisis if older people are empowered to take an active role in the development process.

REFERENCES

Blanchard-Fields, F. and Irwin, J. (1988) The relation between locus of control and coping in two age contexts: Age as a moderator variable. *Psychology and Aging,* 3: 197-203.

Gross, J.J., Carstensen, L. L., Pasupathi, M. Tsai, J. Skorpen, C. G., and Hsu, A.Y.C. (1997) Emotion and aging: Experience, expression, and control. *Psychology and Aging*, 12: 590-599.

James, C. J., and Meredith, W. (1996) Patterns of personality changes across the life span. *Psychology and Aging*, 11: 57-65.

Kanfer, R. & Ackerman, P.L. (2004) Aging, adult development, and work motivation, *Academy of Management Review*, 2004, 29 (3), 440-458.

Ryff, C. D., and Balthes, P. B. (1976) Value transition and adult development in women: The instrumentality-terminality sequence hypothesis. *Developmental Psychology*, 12: 567-568.

Warr, P., Miles, A. and Platts, C. (2001) Age and personality in the British population between 16 and 64 years. *Journal of Occupational and Organizational Psychology*, 74: 165-199.

4

A Socio-Economic Study on Aged Persons in Arunachal Pradesh

—*B. D. Nayak & Shipra Sarkar*

In this world of Globalization and Liberalization, where every effort is made to enrich the quality of human life to cope up with the pace of fast economic development, very little thought is given towards the problems and prospects of the elderly population. Moreover, with increasing expectancy of life, the global aging population is increasing rapidly and according to the projected figures the world will be inhabited by about 2.0 billion people above 60 years of age by 2010 AD and about 75 per cent of them is likely to be in the developing world. In India the problem of aged was not a serious one in some decades earlier but due to socio-economic changes in the wake of urbanization and demographic transition the problem of aging is taking a serious turn both in rural as well as urban sectors and hence it requires serious attention without any delay.

Being scattered in their habitats and unaware about the changes that have been occurring in the society, the tribals in India as well as in North Eastern Region in general and in Arunachal Pradesh in particular, remained socio-economically backward since the dawn of human civilization. Basically, tribe is an aggregate of people sharing social values, common dialect, and territory, usually under a chief and maintaining a distinct cultural trait. Though they form a formidable and an important segment of north eastern economy, they remained away from the mainstream of developmental processes till recent past. However, extension of various facilities regarding education, health, banking, transport and communication in subsequent Five Year Plans eventually have helped the tribal society to fill the gap of socio-economic backwardness in the region in general and in Arunachal Pradesh in specific.

Definition

'Social gerontology' is a distinct discipline of studying problems of old age. The term gerontology has been derived from two Greek words namely "geron" meaning old man and "logy" meaning scientific study. It is that branch of knowledge which is concerned with situations and changes inherent in increment of time with particular reference to post-maturation stage.

The father of gerontology was a medical scientist named Vladimir Kerenchevsky who was the first to recognize that individuals do not die from old age but rather from a pathological interference in the psychological process.

According to concise *Oxford Dictionary* the term ageing means to grow old or show signs of advancing age. The term "elderly", however, is defined as "some what old" passed middle age. Various interpretations are given to the concept of old age.

Various interpretations are given to the concept of old age. For instance the United Nations uses 60 years as the starting point of the elderly group and defines the very old as being 80 plus years old. Whereas A.A.R.P. (American Association of Retired Persons) groups the years of 45-49 as constituting midlife, of 60-74 as older and 75 and more as the very old. Old age varies, however, according to numerous influences on a person, such as life style, health of family status, and cannot be measured by chronological age or by specified retirement age. But in my study I have taken the age mark 60-74 to define as aged and 75 and above as very old.

Future Trend of Aged Persons

With the increasing life expectancy, the global population is aging rapidly and according to the projected figures the world will be inhabited by 2.0 billion people above 60 years of age by 2010 A. D. and about 75 per cent of these are likely to be in the developing world. The detail projections made by the UN Population Division show the massive demographic shift that is taking place in both the developing and developed countries. According to these projections the proportion of the population aged 60 and over in the more developed regions will grow from 18 per cent in 2005 to 22 per cent in 2025. In parallel, the less developed countries will see 11 to 18 per cent by 2025. In the case of India this is estimated to rise from present 10 per cent to 20 per cent in 2025. In absolute numbers, India's aged population will be almost doubled in 2025 if the growth of the general population and medical facilities are developed at presently planned rates.

The tribals of our country constitute an important section of population from anthropological perspective. The population of these Scheduled Tribes as per 2001 census constitutes 8 per cent of the total population of the country. Even today there exist a few studies dealing specifically with the aged tribals of our country.

Implications of increased proportion of elderly people

One implication of the increase in the absolute and relative numbers of older persons in the population is that it will have wide reaching impact on the socio-economic development, including such factors as productivity, consumption, saving and pattern of government expenditure.

A second implication of vital significance lies in the humanitarian sphere, i.e. a concerted effort will be needed to plan services for greatly increased number of older persons. It is clear that higher proportions and growing number of the aged will necessitate fundamental adjustments in economic and social infrastructure. These adjustments which need decades to implement must be initiated now.

Objectives

- To find out the trend of elderly people in Arunachal Pradesh,
- To study the socio-economic profile of the aged persons in the state,

- To analyse the contribution of these people in various spheres,
- To highlight their role in maintaining the social order and preserving the value and culture in the society in general and in their family in specific; and
- To study their problems within and outside their families.

Some Methodological Problems

There has been a paucity of literature and information about the life style of the tribal people living in Arunachal Pradesh. Further, it is felt that the information on scheduled tribes is very scanty, sporadic and sketchy as not to mention to any notable research study. So far the socio-economic aspects of the aged and elderly persons of varied tribal communities are concerned no such noteworthy research is made so far in Arunachal Pradesh.

The present study brings together the salient features of the socio-economic status of elderly people in tribal society of Arunachal Pradesh. A study of their feature affecting their economic and social position cannot be understood and appreciated fully by using the secondary data. To fill this gap, a field survey is conducted to elicit the primary date in certain areas of the state. Thus the present study is based on field survey of some villages/hamlets and surrounding areas of Itanagar Capital city. The 124 numbers of tribal families are covered under the field survey purposively in order to get as many aged persons as possible. Most of the families are composed of parents and their married and unmarried children and grand children. Data for the study were collected with the help of field trip observations, life history, case study and structured interview methods.

Data Analysis

Socio-economic profiles of the Respondents

In the present study the researcher has surveyed 124 aged persons' families covering four major tribes of Arunachal Pradesh. Of the 124 aged respondents sixteen each are belonging to Adi and Galo communities, forty-two are from Apatani and the rest fifty are from Nishi communities (Table-1). The figures in Table-2 show that only seventeen of them are literate having education maximum up to Class V and the rest are illiterate. Majority of them (110) are in the age group of 60–75 years and 14 are very old (75 and more years). Out of 124 respondents 59 are male and 65 are female. About 17 per cent aged persons are dependent while 83 per cent are bread earners. They contribute the family in terms of income and assisting in meeting the financial needs of their families. It is also noticed that majority of them (93 per cent) are consuming wine/local liquor.

It is further seen that majority (60 %) of the aged and elderly persons have their living partners and about 95 per cent of them are staying with their children/grand children while only 2 respondents out of 124 are living with their spouse only.

Table-1
Age Composition of the Surveyed Respondents

Sl. No.	Tribes	60-65	65-70	70-75	75and above	Total
1	Adi	5	4	5	2	16 (13)
2	Apatani	23	10	4	5	42 (34)
3	Galo	5	6	4	1	16 (13)
4	Nishi	25	13	6	6	50 (40)
5	Total	58 (47)	33 (27)	19 (15)	14 (11)	124

Table-2
General Feature of the Surveyed Respondents

Sl. No.	Particulars	No. of Surveyed Respondents	Tribal Groups Adi	Apatani	Galo	Nishi	Total
1	Male	124	12	17	9	21	59 (48)
2	Female	124	4	25	7	29	65 (52)
3	Literate (within Class-V)	124	7	4	4	2	17 (14)
4	Illiterate	124	9	38	12	48	107 (86)
5	Spouse alive	124	9	26	10	32	77 (62)
6	Living with Children	124	14	42	15	47	118 (95)
7	Living with spouse only	124	1	0	1	0	2

Social Status of the Surveyed Respondents

Social problems of the aged and elderly persons in the society are the prime concern of the society irrespective of the caste, creed and religion. As the absolute as well as relative figures of the number of elderly persons are increasing considerably the importance of their well being is gaining utmost priority of the society. It is observed in any non-tribal society that the socio-economic condition and status of the sizeable portion of the population in the society are not at all rosy rather it is degrading day by day. However, unlike the non tribal society, the same of the aged persons in tribal society is relatively better. They command better status and enjoy comparatively better privilege both in the family and in community/clan as because of their co-operative way of living and abundant indigenous knowledge in various fields. They use to get immense respect and care by the younger because of their natural and indigenous medical and ritual knowledge/skill. They are generally treated as the source of knowledge. This study also reveals the similar conclusion. About 76 per cent of the surveyed old persons have opined that they are heard/obeyed by their children in their families but the younger ones (grand children) care them less. However, about cent per cent of them take meal jointly with their children and grand children (Table-4). It is noticed that their role in their community though declines yet they enjoy special status in all celebrities/festivals in their own family. About 85 per cent of them replied affirmatively. So far their health care is concerned, they get all attention from family members, community people and medical practitioners as well.

Contribution of Aged People

Aged people represent an opportunity rather than

crisis, a solution rather than a problem, an asset rather than a burden, a resource rather than a drain on resources and a group that cannot only make an economic contribution, but also that often needs to be the beneficiary of that contribution.

It is important to mention that though these aged persons are least cared for both within and outside the family, still they make many major contributions to the development of their community at large.

(i) ***Income generation***

Any money and effort invested to empower older people through income generation activities will go a long way to develop their confidence and self esteem. This will enable them to spend their last days in happiness and dignity. Almost 83 per cent respondents said that they contribute whatever little possible to the family income. They use to collect various minor forest products from forests and make different types of crafts and sell them in the market in the one hand and manufacture various cloths and household items and enhance the family income by selling them on the other. It is seen in Table-3 that around 79 per cent of the aged people in the state are engaged in collection of minor forest produce in order to assist their family in terms of supplementary income and almost all of the surveyed elderly people in the state produce various household articles out of the forest collections and about 59 per cent of them also go market for selling these items.

(ii) ***Agricultural operation***

Most of the aged persons do varieties of farming

activities not only in their own fields but also in others field on mutual exchange basis. By doing agricultural operation they not only help the family in production but also save the money by reducing the necessity of hired labour for agriculture purpose. They also contribute in terms of transferring farming skill and knowledge to the younger family members in a big way. It is further observed in Table-3 that sizeable percentage of aged people particularly from Apatani community use to go to the field for farm activities as well.

Table-3
Economic Status of the Surveyed Respondents

Sl. No.	Particulars	No. of Surveyed Respondents	Tribal Groups				
			Adi	Apatani	Galo	Nishi	Total
1	Earning Member	124	15	40	16	32	103 (83)
2	Dependent	124	1	2	0	18	21 (17)
3	Pension/any other residual income	124	2	0	1	1	4
4	Agricultural Field work	124	12	29	13	4	58 (47)
5	Collection of minor forest produce	124	13	38	12	35	98 (79)
6	Preparation of crafts and other domestic use articles	124	16	41	16	47	120 (98)
7	Selling of items in market	124	6	25	10	32	73 (59)

Table-4
Social Status of the Surveyed Respondents

Sl. No.	Particulars	No. of Surveyed Respondents	Tribal Groups				
			Adi	Apatani	Galo	Nishi	Total
1	Do the Children listen you?	124	10	31	12	41	94 (76)
2	Do the grand children listen?	124	8	17	6	22	53 (43)
3	Does your spouse care you?	124	9	26	10	32	77 (62)
4	Do you take meal with family members?	124	15	42	15	50	122 (98)
5	Do you play any role in your family at the time of special occasions?	124	13	38	14	41	106 (85)
6	Do you play any role in your community at the time of special occasions?	124	6	7	4	28	45 (36)
7	Does your family care you?	124	12	28	10	35	85 (69)
8	Does your community care you?	124	12	28	10	36	86 (69)

(Contd...)

Sl. No.	Particulars	No. of Surveyed Respondents	Tribal Groups Adi	Apatani	Galo	Nishi	Total
9	Do you get medical care in your house?	124	12	34	14	46	106 (85)
10	Do you get medical care in your society?	124	12	27	10	35	84 (85)
11	Do you get proper medical care from doctors?	124	16	42	16	50	124

(iii) *Caring of younger ones*

With more and more younger persons in the family are entering the labour market or at least being employed gainfully outside their homes, the role of older persons in housekeeping and child care is gaining importance. The caring role of the aged people is not limited to children. They often do not have to nurse the sick in the family, nor is this role restricted to the family but widespread amongst the community.

As many as 97 per cent respondents felt that their involvement in house-keeping and child care is very much necessary for the smooth functioning of family life.

(iv) *Inter-generational communication*

In most of the tribal villages there are no special institutions or mechanisms for the aged to spend their leisure time. It was observed that in wedding and funeral ceremonies, some chit-chats at the streamside or village well or on their way to the farm fields or forest are some of the moments of relaxation for them. Some of them spend their time occasionally by playing with their grand children. A few others sometimes join the gossip group in the evening for refreshment. Thus, the structural mechanisms which the aged people use to cope with their life situation are the patterns of interaction maintained by them within the family, the kin group and the community. It is also seen in Table-5 that about 39 per cent of them get some sort of entertainment in the house itself while 49 per cent aged persons get recreational facility within their village vicinity.

(v) *Environmental protection*

The aged people play a very important role in protecting the environment. About 80 per cent of our respondents felt that deforestation will have a tremendous effect in the tribal way of life. They advise the younger generation to protect the forest by making them aware of the evil effects of deforestation. By telling them folklore and folktale related to environment, they try to communicate the younger generation not to play with nature. It is significant to note that about 55 per cent of our respondents take active part in aforestation activities in their localities.

(vi) *Preserving/maintaining value and culture in the society in general*

It is noticed from the field survey in four selected tribal communities that the aged persons do not like the fast changing scenario in the society. They are fed up with the present trend of social order where there is no time for caring others problems. The young children are also not bothering the aged grand parents and have become more materialistic. They often question their own family/community belief and running after the modern urban culture and way of living. All the surveyed aged people are in the opinion that they find great change in their family because of the modern urban culture. Though it has brought many ease to their life and living style yet they are not happy with this modern style of living and culture. Only 15 per cent of them are in favour of this change and almost all elderly persons are having apprehension that this change will spoil the value system in their indigenous tribal culture resulting in the erosion of their identity.

Problems of Aged People

Though most of our surveyed respondents suffer from one or the other physical problems, still a majority of them undertake certain personal task without the assistance of others. Their diet remains inadequate and unbalanced. Their staple food is rice though most of them are non-vegetarians and they like to have meat but they are unable to afford it except rarely. It is also observed that old people have the same diet as the rest of the family even though the aged, because they eat/ take meal jointly with their children and grand children. Since they tend to eat less, require food of a more nutritious quality which often they don't get.

The consequence of inadequate and low nutrition food intake combined with the extra workload is bound to show on the physical health of the aged people.

Majority of our respondents still depend on ethno medicine and magico-religious practices to counter the physical ailments and diseases.

Table-5
Problems and Facility of the Surveyed Respondents

Sl. No.	Particulars	No. of Surveyed Respondents	Tribal Groups				
			Adi	Apatani	Galo	Nishi	Total
1	Health	124	6	18	3	25	52 (42)
2	Food	124	14	43	10	48	115 (93)
3	Consumption of Alcohol	124	14	43	10	48	115 (93)
4	Financial	124	9	33	11	47	100 (81)
5	Psychological	124	4	15	7	27	53 (43)
6	Entertainment Facility in house	124	7	21	4	16	48 (39)
7	Do you have any recreational facility	124	8	26	15	12	61 (49)

(a) *Economic problems*

All surveyed elderly people, like any other rural poor families, are largely dependent on their daily work for their survival. Only 4 surveyed persons are pension holders. Therefore, they always expect from their family members, irrespective of age, some economic contribution either in cash or in kind. Most of the aged persons undertake field work or collection of forest produce because of their financial need. Thus, they do it not out of choice, but because of the demanding situation. Some of them receive positive while others negative treatment within the family and from the relatives and village people as well.

(b) *Socio-Psychological Problems*

Apart from the aforesaid problems, our res-pondents also experience some socio-psychological problems. One such problem is their decreasing influence on the family members. As many as 85 per cent of the respondents admitted that they are now less influential as compared to their young age. A majority of them play only marginal role in the decision-making process of the family.

At the community level, a majority of our respondents do not play any significant role. However, our respondents frequently receive invitation from their community members to attend various social ceremonies and rituals. The aged respondents again face the problem of the generation gap to a considerable extent. They expressed that on many occasions their opinions vary from those of their younger family members. Having a traditional approach and outlook, they find it difficult to adjust to the new changing social milieu. However, majority of our respondents are in the opinion that they like to stay with their close relatives like sons, daughters and with spouse, they don't like to stay in the community halls if made for them in villages.

Table-6
Observations of Surveyed Respondents

Sl. No.	Particulars	No. of Surveyed Respondents	Tribal Groups				
			Adi	Apatani	Galo	Nishi	Total
1	Do you find any change in your family due to modernization of society?	124	16	42	16	50	124
2	Do you like this change?	124	1	4	5	8	18 (15)
3	Do you like to stay with sons/ daughters?	124	16	42	15	47	120 (97)
4	Do you like to live in old age home?	124	0	0	1	3	4
5	Do you think this change will spoil the value system in the family/ society?	124	16	42	16	48	122 (98)

Coping Mechanisms

The aged persons irrespective of their clan and community draw on their religious sources to cope with their emotional problems. The capacity to adjust to the difficult situations of their life is enhanced by their belief in the concept of *Karma* which governs the attitude of life of the aged people. To cope with events that bring about emotional stress, the tendency of the aged tribals is to have recourse to spiritual healers and practitioners of traditional medicine.

Conclusion

The gradual change in their habitat has minimized the dependence on nature and the supernatural. But this change has not in anyway promoted their primitive socio-economic conditions of life. They still continue to roam about in the forests in search of food, hunting, fishing, rope making materials, basketry, house building materials, fuelwood, medicinal herbs, plants and numerous minor forest products like honey, resin and other edible oils, etc.

While they cling to their old and cherished values, their children learn to take for granted the changing social environment. Hence it creates a more pronounced generation gap between aged and elderly people and their younger family members.

5

Problems of the Aged in Arunachal Pradesh: Reflections

—Tado Karlo

[In this autobiographic reflections, the plight of the aged is highlighted with special reference to Arunachal Pradesh. In a transient society, the problem of old people is seen to be acute. The first hand account of a tribal has been brought out in the form a case study. Policy intervention is needed to provide sufficient space for the senior citizens in the present socio-political setup. The inevitability of old age and death in every one's life could be used as a tool to improve the conditions of the aged. The communication gap between the younger and the older generations need to be bridged for a better future].

My grand mother was 75 when she died. I saw her off when she left this world. It took about a year for her to pass away from our dwellings. I was just studying in 3rd standard and walked 7 kilometres one way to go to my school. In spite of my daily walk of 14 kilometres and home works at home, I had to get up in the middle of the winter nights to attend to my ailing grandmother's need for help. She used to call my mother and father also for help. They would in turn call me out and finally, it used to be me who would get up, light the fire place, serve her hot tea with biscuits or give her medicine or help her sit up or give her support for easing herself or support her in any other way. I used to wash her clothes and remove the louses from her hair and clothes. Other family members were fed up with her prolonged illness.

It appeared to me that time that no body wanted to invest in a dying old lady. To me it was philosophy: I did not expect any thing from her. I simply wanted to share her last days and give my best to her. As a child, I virtually experienced the transition of life into death by remaining close to her for about a year just before she died. At one point of time, she could not go to the toilet without my support. Later, she had to do bowl cleaning while sitting where she was. After some time, she could not even get up. She could only roll on the sides. A stage came when she could not move her body parts freely. Then a time came, when she laid herself stretched but still breathing. Finally, she stopped breathing. I was the only one who saw her breathing the last.

Ever since, I have always looked at every aged person as a bridge between life and death. That is how, old people have inspired awe in me and I have had the good company of number of agerians, in my later life and received lots of support from them.

Perhaps, the support I received from agerians came due to the blessing from the spirit of my grandmother. My friendship with the older generation paid me back in number of ways.

C.D. Radhakrisnan: I met him in a train when he

was returning from pilgrimage. I had a long association with him, throughout my college and university days. I used to regularly visit him at his residence at Narasimhapuram and later, at Triplicane, when I was doing my graduation in Madras. I used to send Hamdard medicine to him from Delhi, when I shifted to Delhi for further studies.

M.O. Srinivasan: A former Test cricketer, he used to keep his days busy by taking music classes. I had deep regard for this old man and he once invited me to a lunch at his residence, when I was just a college student. He must have been 70 plus.

N. Gopalaswamy: A former Major General of Indian National Army. I had the good company of this man and had the privilege of having daily food for number of months. He was 76 years old at that time.

B.K. Royburman: Prof. Royburman, 85 years old, is a moving spirit in the Indian scene. I have the privilege of his occasional company since 1994. He is the one who advised Mrs. Indira Gandhi to set up NERIST in North East India. He was Chairman of ICSSR.

He has been Chairmen of number of National Level Commissions and Committees. Presently, he is the Chairman of Commission for Review of Environmental and Social Sector Policy, Govt. of Sikkim. He is also the Chairman of Committee for Social Impact Assessment of Asian Highway and Trans-border Trade, Govt. of India, of which I am a member.

When my mother died on June 24, 2006 at the age of 65, few days later, I dreamt that she was packing up her luggage for a train journey to South India all alone. She was going there permanently to some unknown destination. This is one reason for reliving my Madras days. In the dream I told her to maintain cleanliness as she would be traveling alone in the train. I saw that other passengers in her compartment were old people clad in white.

My mother died of neglect. She was rooted to the village. Except one of our brothers, all of us work in different parts of Arunachal Pradesh. We have two sisters, both married and do not stay at home. One of our brothers, who could not go for higher education and settled in the village, is in charge of the village home. This brother had a feeling of being left behind and did not look after our mother. We invited her to stay with any one of us. However, her attachment to the village was stronger and she remained there. She could not have adjusted herself with the urban setting at our places any way. She died due to lack of proper health care and timely attention, typical of rural areas and also due to the indifference of the one who was supposed to attend to her at the time of distress.

Few months after my mother's death, an old man committed suicide. He was 75 plus. In the evening he packed his belongings. In the early morning he dressed himself in the best possible way. He hanged himself just sitting on his bed. He could have survived if he had a second thought to survive. But he had none. The reason: the burden of old age was too much and he did not want to bother any one. He was a grand uncle of mine. He was going strong physically except for the weak eyesight. I had asked him to come down to my place for cataract operation. But his preoccupations in the village and the physical distance proved to be too costly. He was clinging to his village and not so much to his life.

In my childhood, I have witnessed an old man and an old woman starved to death in two different families at different times. Our way to the school passed through a village. We could hear the old man crying for food while passing by one of the houses, till his death. He was discarded by his son and other younger relatives. In my own village, an old woman died due to starvation after she broke her hand due to an accident and became invalid. Her family members neglected her. In another instance, an old man from a neighbouring house used to live with us. He was alone and used to shift places as ever known every family saw him as a liability. He was a refugee of time.

When my time came for marriage, it was a hard choice. I wanted at least a graduate girl well versed in my mother tongue and with expertise in traditional cooking. It was hard to find one. Most of the educated girls, particularly those coming from affluent families, could not speak in mother tongue and those good in tribal cooking were harder to find. I wanted some one who would be conversant with my old parents and understand their needs. The choice was between one who would be compatible with my parents but not so much with me intellectually; and the other, who would be incompatible with my parents but intellectually compatible with me. At last, I went for the former. I went for an undergraduate girl coming from a humbler village background and thereby reduced the cultural gap between her and my old parents. Otherwise, my parents would have felt isolated in my house.

Often, it is not the communication gap due to cultural difference that decides the plight of the old and aged in the society. In my wife's village, an old couple lived with their lone son. After his wife's death, the old man was seen as a burden by his son and daughter-in-law. The old man was known for his hunting ability. As long as he brought back something from hunting, the daughter-in law used to feed him well. However, hunting or fishing being seasonal, he could not pay for his food every time in terms of his catches. He used to carry fuel wood in return for the food at other times. Fed up with the ill treatment met out to him by his daughter-in-law and son, he exiled himself in the deep mountain, about 10 kilometres from the village. In a month's time, once or twice he used to come down to his village to exchange his catches for rice. Once, my wife's mother sensed that something was wrong with the old man: he did not come to the village for a month. She mobilized the villagers to go in search of the old man. No body knew his exact location. They had to hunt for him and finally found him seriously ill. He had been lying on one side of his body for weeks, unable to move. As a result, a hole was formed between the ribs. The villagers brought him down to the village where he died after a month.

In recent time, I have seen two old couple, who had their graves prepared before hand and at the same place side by side, separated only by a partition. A window was made in the partition and a single cover was made for the two graves. However, when it was realized later that the two may not die on the same day, the window was closed and separate lids were prepared for the graves. They got flowers planted around the graves. They were sure that they will die and but they were not sure whether the children will prepare their graves to their liking. The older generation has lost faith in the younger generation. There is a need to instill a feeling of security in the older generation.

There is a selfishness of generation that is creating a wider generation gap in terms of communication and concern for the weaker. The present generation is not concerned about the future generation. When the present generation becomes old, the younger generation does not think beyond its immediate needs. This is particularly true in the case of Arunachal Pradesh. Be it environment, economy or ethics, the materialistic outlook of the advancing wave of humanity seems to be inherited by the succeeding wave.

In Arunachal, the younger generation is slowly and steadily gaining control over the politics. The contributions of the veterans are not counted. The political culture in the state has shaped the character of its citizens. The electoral politics looks for immediate and short term gains. It encourages short term memory and counts on materialistic benefits alone. The senior citizens are the victims of the present day setup. Their past contributions and experiences are not counted. Their wisdom has no value in the new value system.

My father belongs to the first batch of pioneer leaders in Arunachal Pradesh. He was one of the Agency

Councilors of NEFA Council and is the lone survivor among the former Councilors. He has been a Panchayat leader at the highest level of local self government for a long time. However, now-a-days, when election time comes, there seems to be a consensus on candidature: put up a younger candidate. This is how older generation is being phased out thereby making them insignificant and irrelevant politically and hence, socially.

When I took my ailing father to Madras, the TTE asked for proof of my father's claim for railway concession as a senior citizen. The fact is that there cannot be any proof. My grandparents did not have any record. When he told the TTE that he had witnessed the major earthquake of 1950 as a young boy, TTE was not impressed. How does one get the proof of being a senior citizen in Arunachal Pradesh?

Of late, I have found that an aged person is also a bridge between the past and present. It is increasingly realized by many that the older people, particularly, the priests and experts in indigenous knowledge, are a treasure for the community and their knowledge and wisdom should be recorded and documented. Old can still be gold. With this hopeful and optimistic note, it is hoped that a system will be put in place to take proper care of the old, with the expectation that when one grows old, this very system will give shelter to the worn and torn.

The problem of the aged is an age old problem. Among the solutions to this problem, existing and other possible ones, the following can be considered:

1. *Reservation for the old (60 plus) in politics*: Political empowerment of any weaker section of the society is considered as a solution to most of the problems of that section. While the existing political setup does not put a bar on the upper age limit for political participation, there is no reservation for the aged in elections. If reservation exists for other weaker sections, it should also be considered for senior citizens. Their political status will ensure them socio-economic status.

2. *Multi-skill development for survival*: After retirement, those who have multi-skills can continue to keep themselves busy and active. They continue to have social utility and therefore, survive better. A multi-skill development strategy can help minimize the problems of old age.

3. *Senior Citizen's Club*: Loneliness seems to be a major problem in old age: Govt. sponsored clubs with recreation facilities could help them out of loneliness and isolation.

6

Ageing Population in Arunachal Pradesh – A Comparative Study

—R.P. Bhattacharjee

With the advancement of societies, the process of ageing has become more rapid in the developed countries and has started leaving an impact on the developing countries. Until about 200 years ago, the age structure of various populations did not differ much. All the countries had typical pyramid-shaped age structures representative of high fertility and high mortality. With the advancement of societies ushered in by industrialization and technological progress, the age structure of developed countries experienced substantial changes. Their populations have become older, or in other words, proportion of older persons has markedly increased. This process of increase in the proportion of elderly persons and decrease in the proportion of children is known as 'ageing' of population. The conventional bell-shape of the pyramid changes to a barrel-like shape with a smaller base and a comparatively broader apex. This process has been evident in most of the developed countries. Their populations become progressively older upto 1950s and this trend has continued despite the increase in birth rates experienced by some of these countries during 1940s and 1950s (IIPS, 1994).

The ageing problem has been growing in developing countries in recent years as a social problem for policy makers and as a result old age pension and other social measures are being taken in developing countries including in India.

In the North Eastern States, the ageing problem in increasing due to low death rate and increasing life expectancy. For example, the birth rates of Arunachal Pradesh was 36.8 in 1971 which decreased to 32.1 during 1981 in rural areas while it was 30.9 during 1991 but decreased further to 20.2 (combined) during 2002 (NEC, 2006). Similarly, the death rate of this state was 19.8 during 1971 and this sharply decreased to only 4.8 during 2002. The decrease of birth rate and death rate is almost similar in this region. The life expectancy of the country has increased sharply during last few decades.

But there is no sufficient data on smaller state including in this North Eastern Region. The author had estimated the life expectancy of Arunachal Pradesh as 54.4 (Bhattacharjee, 2000) and life expectancy is also estimated by the Rajiv Gandhi University as 54.05 in the first ever Human Development Report (APHDR, 2005). Here, because of low life expectancy, the ageing population in the state is not severe. This is discussed at later part of this paper.

Ageing Problems

There are marked geographical differences in the current ageing pattern. The elderly persons constitute less than 3% of the total population in Africa, particularly Eastern and Western areas. At the other end of the spectrum are Northern Europe and Western Europe where the proportion of aged 65 or over is about 15%. The populations of Eastern Europe and the then USSR are relatively younger than those of the other developed countries. In Latin America and Asia, the proportion of aged 65 or over is about 5%.

Most of the developed countries have higher proportion of aged 65 or over as compared to the developing and the least developed countries. They experienced rapid development characterized by the expansion and application of modern techniques to primary sector activities, namely, agricultural and raising of livestock. Per Capita Income and Savings are much higher. Mortality has reduced and levels of educational attainment have risen considerably. It is evident from our earlier discussion that the process of ageing is faster in the developed countries as compared to the developing countries. It, therefore, emerges as a problem more for developed countries.

One of the most important problems of the elderly is their economic dependence. The most comprehensive source of income for them is the state administered social security system that provided retirement benefits and pensions. This proportion of the elderly population is expected to grow continuously. A very small proportion of the total elderly population does not receive these benefits.

Another problem is related to their living arrangement, which may vary over time and place, depending upon such economic and social factors as availability of housing, population distribution between urban and rural areas, family structure, social norms and customs. With the break-up of the joint family system, a growing proportion of elderly population has started staying in the "Old age homes" or private institutions or nursing homes. For example, in 1989 based on the monograph prepared by the Madras Institute of Ageing, called "Care for the Elderly", 15,471 elderly were accommodated in old age homes around the country. In 1995, HelpAge's survey of 256 old age homes, as presented in its national directory of old age homes, found only 12,702 residents in all old age homes in India, even though there was simultaneous demand for more beds (Shankardass, 2000). Not all of these were under the government and were founded by religious organizations, private sources and other types of trusts and caste organizations. In fact, the government seeks active participation of the voluntary sector to meet the needs of older persons.

Significantly, healthcare as social security does not seem to exist in any state. This is alarming given the fact that the growth rate of the 60 and above age group is higher than that of other age groups. Older people's healthcare needs are of much concern given the inadequate provisions in the public sector and the prohibitive costs for private healthcare (Gopal, 2006).

In the more advanced age, susceptible to illness, care from the family members is expected. Nursing duties like feeding, cleaning and administration of medication are required to be rendered. Large families are more equipped to cope with these tasks than small families. However, mostly in urban areas where small families are often the norm, all family members frequently work, it is becoming more socially acceptable to hire home care personnel or institutionalize elderly members. Nevertheless, nursing homes are still perceived as the last resort by a majority of the population.

Although, population ageing does not emerge as severe a problem for developing countries as it has in the developed countries, the need to care for the elderly has been accepted and organized. Since efforts are being made within the economic scope of the governments to launch various programmes for the purpose (IIPS, *ibid*).

Ageing Concern in India

Older people, and in particular, older women are an extremely marginalized group of people, who hardly merit the attention of state protection. As women, they occupy a position, which is more disadvantaged than older men, and older people the additional vulnerability of dependency and support from others. In both instances, their contribution both economically and socially to the household and community is hardly recognized. Demographically, populations are displaying an aged complexion across the world. In terms of aggregate population in India, the proportion of elderly, those above 60 years of age, was 5.4% of the total population in 951 numbering 2 crores and it had increased to 6.7% in 1991 totaling to 5.7 crores. The rate of growth of the population of this age group has also been higher than that of others contributing to its increasing proportion in the overall population. Further, the proportion of women in the 60 + age group is higher than the male population (Bose, 2000). The number, proportion and sex ratio of elderly in India by age groups is shown in Table 1.

Table-1

Number, Proportion and Sex Ratio of Elderly in India by Age Groups 1961-2001

1. No. in crores

No. of crores	60+	70+	80+	Age Group 90+	110+
1	2	3	4	5	6
1961	2.5	0.9	0.2	0.05	0.001
1971	3.3	1.1	0.3	0.07	0.001
1981	4.3	1.5	0.4	0.07	0.001
1991	5.7	2.1	0.6	0.10	0.001
2001	7.7	2.9	0.8	#	0.001
2. Percentage to Total Population					
1961	5.6	2.0	0.6	0.1	0.02
1971	6.0	2.1	0.6	0.1	0.02
1981	6.49	2.33	0.62	0.1	0.02
1991	6.76	2.51	0.76	0.2	0.02
2001	7.5	2.9	0.8	#	#
3. Sex Ratio					
1971	1066	1030	950	897	798
1981	1042	1026	990	892	844
1991	1075	1084	1090	1019	896
2001	1028	991	1051	#	#

#-Not available

Source: Irudaya Rajan,"Population Ageing and Health in India", Cehet, Mumbai, July 2006 (Compiled from Tables 1 and 2)(Cited from Gopal, 2006).

Here, in this Table 1 we find that the sex ratio of 60+ is very high and leads to the conclusion that the old age women needs special care than old age men.

In response to the growing change in age composition and faster ageing, the centre and state governments in India have for past few years been engaged in drawing a set of policy initiatives to help the older persons. Also, there have been commitments by the Government at various national and international forums to assimilate the growing number of aged in the process of development. Internationally, this commitment was particularly more resounding in the UN Sponsored Second World Assembly on Ageing in Madrid (Spain) held in April, 2002. At the national level, besides some direct measures of protective subsidies and income transfers, the Union Government has also drawn a National Policy on Older Person (NPOP) in January 1999. This policy, apparently designed without an in-depth analysis of the ageing scenario over the coming years or a detailed situational assessment of the country's aged, underscores the need for public initiatives in areas of financial security, health care, nutrition, shelter, education, welfare and protection of life and property of the aged. Despite these commitments and policy guidelines, some of the more recent literature on issues of ageing reveals very high physical and financial dependence faced by the aged in India (Alam, 2004).

Old age is the time for persons to relax and enjoy the fruits of their hard labour during early life. But in most of the less developed countries including India, where the aged, who unlike their counterparts in more developed countries, live in abject poverty in the absence of old age pension and other social security programmes and insufficient personal savings. In addition, lower fertility, on the one hand, results in fewer children to look after the old parents and on the other hand, many of these children move away from their family in search of livelihood elsewhere. Further, recent decline in mortality increased the longevity of the old persons in general and women in particular, result in an increase in the number of older persons who are in need of both financial and familial support. Besides these, the process of urbanization tends to increase the number of nuclear families and bring about numerous changes in life styles not only among the young but also among the aged (Audinarayan, 2001).

Ageing Population in Arunachal Pradesh

Arunachal Pradesh has total population of 10,97,968 as per 2001 population census while there is population of 20, 000 of age 60-64 and population age 65 and above is 29,916 (DES, 2006). Thus ageing population in this State is 2.7% of total population. The ageing-index in Arunachal Pradesh during 2001 is 7.01. Thus ageing population in this state cannot be ignored and proper planning is required based on experience gathered of whole of India and the World. The ageing population of Arunachal Pradesh during last few census decades is shown in table 2.

Table-2
Ageing population of Arunachal Pradesh (1981-2001)

Age Group	1981	1991	2001
Total Population	631,839	864,558	1097,968
Male	339,322	465,004	579,941
Female	292,517	399,554	518,027
60-64 Total Population	30,093 (60+)	16,790	20,000
Male	16,264	9,447	10,707
Female	13,829	7,343	9,293
Rural	29,543	16,039	18,275
Male	15,948	8,984	9,722
Female	13,595	7,055	8,553
Urban	550	751	1,725
Male	316	463	985
Female	234	288	740
65+ Total	550	20,770	29,916
Male	316	11,130	15,710
Female	234	9,640	14,206
Rural	550	19,860	27,698
Male	316	10,631	14,541
Female	234	9,219	13,157
Urban	550	910	2,212
Male	316	499	1,169
Female	234	421	1,049

Source: (1) Census of India, 1981,1991 & 2001

In Table 2, the elderly population of 1981 is for whole of 60+ population as data is not available. We find that the ageing population is not much in urban areas and it is mainly in rural areas that all the ageing people are concentrated in this state. The sex ratio of ageing population during 2001 is 904 and due to this, all plans and programme of this state should be both for male and female equally without any deprivation. 92.3% of ageing population is leaving in rural areas of this state. Thus ageing problem, if any, lies in rural areas of the state. The Old age pension of the department of social welfare should be targeted in rural areas mainly. It may be mentioned that old age pension of Rs75/- per month is paid to those above 65 years of age while Rs.150/- is paid to those who are 60-65 ages. The number of such pensions in the state at the end of 31st March 2004 was 1555 for the age group of 60-65 and 13,500 for the age group above 65 years (DES, 2004). Thus, total coverage of old age pension is hardly 30 % of total 60+ elders in this state. The achievement of old-age pension during 2003-2004 was 1500 while during 2004-2005; it was 1666 only (Draft, AOP, 2005-2006).

The ageing population in Arunachal Pradesh needs proper health care facilities. During 2001, the certificate of death due to tuberculosis to male was 2 between age group of 65-69, while 4 Nos. of death recorded to 70 years and above. Female Nos of death due to Tuberculosis was only 3. Thus death to female due to this disease is compared to male. The death due to Protozoal diseases like malaria was 3 male and 2 female of age 65-69 while there was occurrence of 1 male dealth due to meningities. The death due to heart diseases recorded much more and it was 7 for male and 9 for females. There was reporting of death due to asthma of 3 male and 2 female while diseases like liver was 2 male and 2 female. The total death report of age 65+ was 179 out of 1032 death reported (DES, 2001). It may be mentioned that registration of death is not much popular in the state as we find that there is very low issue of death certificates but it should be made popular.

Besides census, we have another set of data which is more reliable and this is National Family Health Survey, 1992-93 (known as NFHS-1) and 1998-99 (NFHS-2). The report of third series of NFHS-3 during 2005-2006 is not readily available.

The comparative study of ageing population in Arunachal Pradesh based on NFHS-1 is shown in Table 3.

Table-3
Percentage distribution of ageing population (1992-93)– a study of NER

tate (60-64)	Age group (65+)	
Arunachal Pradesh	2.2 (4)	2.6 (5)
Assam	2.3 (3)	3.6 (3)
Manipur	2.7 (2)	4.1 (2)
Meghalaya	1.6 (6	2.0 (6)
Mizoram	1.7 (5)	3.3 (4)
Nagaland	1.1 (7)	1.2 (7)
Tripura	2.9 (1)	5.5 (1)
India	3.0	4.8

Source: NFHS-1, 1992-93, Introductory Report, IIPS, Mumbai, P-16.

From the first Report of Natianal Health and Family Survey, 1992-93, we find that Tripura had highest ageing population (5.5 %) with rank one (1) while Manipur had ageing population of 4.1 % with rank two (2) and Assam third (3) with ageing population of 3.6%. Arunachal Pradesh had 2.6% of ageing population with rank five (5). The percentage of elderly population of age group of 60-64, we find Tripura had highest percentage of 2.9% with rank one (1) while Manipur and Assam had rank 2 and 3. Arunachal Pradesh had fourth rank of elderly population with 2.2% of ageing population.

Now let us examine the second report of NFHS-2 in table below.

Table-4
Percentage distribution of ageing population (1998-99) of six NE States

State	Age structure	
	(60-64)	(65+)
Arunachal Pradesh	2.0 (6)	3.1 (6)
Manipur	2.4 (2)	4.7 (2)
Meghalaya	2.1 (4)	3.4 (5)
Mizoram	2.3 (3)	4.3 (4)
Nagaland	2.1 (4)	4.4 (3)
Tripura	2.5 (1)	5.2 (1)

Source: NFHS-2, 1998-99, P-18, IIPS, Mumbai

In the above table, we find that percentage of ageing population in six North Eastern State during 1998-99. Tripura had highest percentage of ageing population similar to NFHS-1 while Arunachal Pradesh had least percentage of ageing population among the six North Eastern States (Assam data is not available with the author).

Conclusion

In Arunahcal Pradesh, we find that the ageing population is not acute and it is much less compared to other NE States. But considering about 30,000 ageing population as per 2001 population census, the government should have proper planning for them specially for their health care facilities. My discussion with local friends from the tribes of Apatani, Nishyi, Galo, Adi, Tangsa etc, it is found that the aged members of respective tribes live with their children and grand-children even in the present trend of migration from rural areas urban areas. In few cases, if the dependent children are not available with them, the clan and other community members take care of them in their day to day requirements / works. There are a few instances of old-age people among the indigenous population who need special care in their economic status during ageing period. Many of them are not getting old age pension and a few of them are not getting due amount. The old age pension scheme should cover all ageing population in this developing State. There must be social awareness about their problems. Both the Government and NGOs should come forward to ease the problem, if any. Some of the NGOs have started to take care of destitute and helpless. We may cite the works of "Achukuru Welfare Society's Mother's Home at Ziro who are rendering welfare services to the society in taking care of the destitute and the helpless. More NGOs should come forward to find the problems of the ageing population, if any, especially to budge the loneliness, their economic problems and health care.

REFERENCES

1. International Institute for Population Science (IIPS): *Population Dynamics-II*, Reading Material for MPS, p. 20.
2. North Eastern Council (2006): *Basic Statistics of North Eastern Region*, pp. 166-167, Shillong-3.
3. Bhattacharjee, Dr.R.P. (2000): *Economic Development of Arunachal Pradesh*, Himalayan Publishers, Delhi/Itanagar, p. 230.
4. Arunachal Pradesh Human Development Report, (APHDR), 2005, p. 46.
5. Shankardass, Mala Kapur (2000): "Societal Responses", *Seminar*, p. 488.
6. Gopal, Meena (2006):"Gender, Ageing and Social Security", *Economic and Political Weekly*, Vol.XLI, No.42,p. 4477.
7. Bose, Ashish (2000): "Demographic Transition", *Seminar*, No. 488.
8. Alam,Moneer (2004): "Ageing, Old Age Income Security and Reforms" (An Exploration of Indian Situation), *Economic and Political Weekly*, Vol.XXXIX, No.33,p. 3731.
9. Audinarayana,N (2001):"Factors Affecting the Work Participation of Elderly: An Empirical Investigation", *Demography India*, Vol.30, No.p. 61.
10. Directorate of Economics and Statistics (2006): *Statistical Abstract of Arunachal Pradesh,* 2005, Government of Arunchal Pradesh, Itanagar, p. 20.
11. Census of India, 1981, Series-25, Arunachal Pradesh, Part-III-A&B & part-IV-A, General Economic Tables and Social Cultural Tables, p. 81.
12. Census of India, Arunachal Pradesh, Series-3, Social & Cultural Tables, p. 14.

13. Directorate of Economics and Statistics (2004): "Economic Review of Arunachal Pradesh, 2004", Government of Arunachal Pradesh, Itanagar, p. 58.

14 Department of Planning," Draft Annual Plan, 2005-2006", Government of Arunachal Pradesh, Itanagar, p. 97.

15. Directorate of Economics and Statistics (2001): "Annual Report on the Working of the Registration of Births and Deaths Act, 1969 for the year, 2001", Government of Arunachal Pradesh, Itanagar, pp. 21-26.

16. International Institute for Population Science (IIPS), NFHS-1, 1992-93,P-16and NFHS-2, 1998-99,p. 18.

7

The Problems of Aged and Elderly in Indigenous Communities of Arunachal Pradesh

—S.J. Neethirajan & D.S. Sworna Latha

Introduction and Statement of the Problems

The present study is an attempt to assess the problems of the aged and elderly in indigenous communities of North East India with Special Reference to Arunachal Pradesh. The work goes especially in to the existing problems of the aged, Socio-economic and sociocultural problem of the same. There are no many studies in the diversion of evaluating and accessing the existing problems of the aged and elderly in indigenous communities of Arunachal Pradesh. It is due to inadequate statistical information of the household level. One could note that it is an essential to study about the problems of the aged and Senior Citizens of the state. This study attempts to make an assessment of various problems of the aged and elderly in indigenous communities of North East India with special reference to Arunachal Pradesh, which is necessary information from the policy angle for working out a plan for the aged and elderly.

Research Design

The research design of the study spelling out the objectives, methods of data collection and analysis in detail.

Objectives

1. To access the socioeconomic characteristics of the aged.
2. To study the problems of the aged and elderly in indigenous communities of North East India with special reference to Arunachal Pradesh.

Methodology

The study has been made with reference to three blocks–Doimuk-Pamumpare District, Ziro block - Lower Subansiri District, Pasighat-East Siang District. The rationale behind the choice of these block of the study can be felt out further.

The complexion of the population in these blocks are predominantly dominated by a particular community.

1. Doimuk-Nishi
2. Ziro-Apatani, Hari, Hija.
3. Pasighat-Adi, Rani, Sille.

The different stages are:

Ist stage: Selection of three districts from the State.

IInd stage: Selection of two villages from each block.

IIIrd stage: Selection of ten respondents from each village.

Total sixty respondents had been chosen.

The age of the respondent is an important social variable for influencing the opinion and perception of the respondents towards new ideas and values. And hence an age wise analysis of the respondent is considered to be necessary to carryout the present study. The information related to age wise distribution of the respondents is furnished.

As per the dictionary meaning of the terminology 'elderly' the researchers have started the classification from the age group of 50 years they are grouped into five categories–50-55 ,55-60 ,60-65 ,65-70 and 75 and above

Age-wise classification

Age of the respondents	Emchi	Mani	Hari	Hija	Rani	Sille	Total
50-55	4	3	4	3	3	5	22 (36.66)
55-60	3	4	4	4	5	3	23 (38.33)
60-65	1	2	1	2	1	-	7 (11.66)
65-70	1	1	1	-	1	2	6 (10)
70 and above	1	-	-	1	-	-	2(3)

Note: Figures in parentheses indicate the percentage.

The researchers have gathered the information from sixty respondents and they highly motivated to furnish various personal details required.

The researchers have identified 22 problems about the aged and elderly in the national level and international level. Researcher has made attempts among the aged and elderly in indigenous communities of North East India with special reference to Arunachal Pradesh.

Among the chosen 60 respondents, the following problems were identified under 5 heads as Elderly abuse, Psychological, Health, Economic and Socio-Cultural problems.

Problems of the Aged and Elderly of Arunachal Pradesh

Elderly Abuse	Psychological	Health	Economical	Socio-Cultural
Physical abuse (0)	Self neglect (0)	Ill health (43.3)	Financial constraints (23)	Effect of modernisation (41.6)
Neglect(5)	Emotional & psychological abuse(5)	Poor condition (40)	Unbalanced diet (40)	Neglecting mother tongues (53.2)
Abandonment (0)	Loneliness (10)	Inadequate preventive and curative medical practices(40)		Lack of communication with their grand children (50)
				Deterioration of indigenous culture (60)
Financial and material exploitation (16)	Depression (10)			Changing food habits (23)
	Losing self confidence & will power(6.6)			Less of identity & recognition (o)
				Less importance for religious activities (56)
				Declining moral value (40)

Note: Figures in parentheses indicate the percentage.

I. Elderly Abuse

Physical Abuse, Neglect, abandonment financial and material exploitation were the problems accessed under the head of elderly abuse. Among the 60 respondents no case of physical abuse or abandonment were reported. But 5% of the respondents reported negligence from the family side and 16% of the respondents are facing financial and material exploitation.

The block wise classification goes like this. Nearly 5% of the respondents are facing neglect from their family side in all the three chosen blocks. And financial & material exploitation is reported from 15%, 10% and 25% of the respondents from Doimuk, Ziro and Pasighat blocks respectively.

II. Psychological problems

Self neglect, emotional abuse, loneliness, depression, losing confidence and will power were the problems focused under psychological problems.

Among the chosen 60 respondents, no case of self-neglect has been reported 11% of the respondents have been identified with loneliness and depression and 5% of the respondents are facing emotional abuse and nearly 6.6% of the respondents are losing self-confidence and will Power.

The block wise distribution of this problem shows the following figures: 5% of the respondents are facing emotional abuse in all the three blocks. Nearly 10% of the people are facing the problems of loneliness in Doimuk and Ziro block and 15% of the respondents are facing the problems of depression in all the three blocks.

Among the 6.6% of the respondents who lose their self confidence and will power is distributed as 5% each in Doimuk block, Ziro block and 10% in Pasighat block.

III. Health-related problems

Nearly 43.5% of the respondents of Arunachal Pradesh are facing the problems of ill health. And about 40% of the respondents are suffering from poor sanitary conditions. In addition to that 40% of the respondents have reported about the inadequate preventive and curative medical practices.

The block-wise distribution shows that in Doimuk block, nearly 45% of the respondents are having ill health and in Pasighat nearly 40% of the respondents are facing the problem of ill health. Poor sanitary condition is reported among 40% of the respondents in Doimuk, Ziro block and 45% in Pasighat block.

The problem of inadequate preventive and curative medical practices are sound as 35% in Doimuk block, 40% in Ziro block and Pasighat block each, here the researcher wants to add one fact that the aged and elderly of the indigenous communities in Arunachal Pradsh are having faith upon their indigenous curative methods.

IV. Economic problems

Under the head of economic problems since major group of the chosen respondents comes under low income, groups the problems of financial constraints and unbalanced diet were focussed.

And nearly 23.5% of the respondents are visualising

financial constraints as a problem and 40% of the respondents are not getting balanced diet.

The block-wise classification figures out the following facts 25% of the respondents in Doimuk block and 15% of the respondents in Ziro block and 20% of the respondents from Pasighat block are viewing financial constraints as a problem.

And about 45.5% of the respondents from Doimuk 40% of the respondents from Ziro and 355 of the respondents from Pasighat block an suffering from the problems of unbalance diet.

V. Socio-cultural problems

The Socio-cultural problem includes the effect of modernisation, neglecting mother-tongue, lack of communication with the grandchildren, changing food habits, loss of identity and recognition, less importance for religious activities and declining moral values. In addition, this head of problems is predominant among the aged and elderly in indigenous communities of Arunachal Pradesh.

Nearly 41% of the respondents are not able to cope up with the modernization, 53% of the respondents are suffering because of the neglect of mother-tongue. Nearly 50% of the respondents are not able to communicate with their grand-children, 60% of the respondents are not happy about the diminishing of the indigenous culture and 23% of the respondents suffer because of the changing food habits in their house-hold members. 56% of the respondents are concerned about the declining importance for religious activities and nearly 40.5% are worrying about loss of identity and recognition.

Summary and Conclusion

The discussion above could portray a broad picture of the problems of the aged and elderly in indigenous communities of Arunachal Pradesh. Apart from presenting certain statistical details as to the actual problems, the views entertained by the respondents have also been summarized. The latter is important in view of the fact that the aged and elderly people are highly respected by their family members as well as by their society, because they play very important role in the decision-making task of their family. Their role in performing ritual and puja inevitable. They play vital role in the judiciary systems of their communities. The percentage of psychological problems is found low because the level of expectation and anxiety is low among the aged and elderly here.

The problems of the elderly in indigenous of North East India with special reference to Arunachal Pradesh mainly falls on the socio-cultural problems followed by health and economic problems.

Modernisation and scientific advancement is good but it should not fail to protect their indignities culture and identity. Health facilities should be made available in every village, awareness and popular participation is the need of the hour.

REFERENCES

1. S.D. Jha, *The Wealth of Arunachal Pradesh.*
2. *Statistical Abstract*, Government of Arunachal Pradesh.
3. Internet Sources.

8

Globalization and Future of Ageing in an Indigenous Society

—*Pratul Joshi*

[This paper tries to look into the challenges before ageing people belonging to indigenous society created by the rise of globalization].

India, in the last two decades, has experienced tremendous changes in every field due to the impact of globalization. The process of globalization has increased disparity between the countries as well as within the nation. Globalization has produced a distinctive stage in the social history of ageing. Thus the old structures are being replaced by the new ones either in a modified form or in a completely new avatar.

The indigenous societies are no exception to this change. They have transformed and are still under the process of transformation. The impact of Globalization is much more in these societies because the rate of change was more rapid than in any other society.

Indigenous societies are known for their self-supporting systems. They maintained their distinctive identity because of their life style which included limited needs for survival, their limited exposure and contact with the outer world and also for limited aspirations. The community feeling is a strong force, which bound these societies over the years.

The onslaught of globalization in recent years has created a set of conditions where the existing social fabric underwent tremendous changes. The younger generation is facing entirely different environment. The new environment created by globalization, has put a set of conditions where the break from the past was imminent. The cost of this charge was to be borne by none other than the age-old people.

I am not an aboriginal of this land and my stay in Arunachal is only of 2 and half years. So I cannot claim to be a minute observer of Arunachalee society. But still the nature of problem is almost same as in other part of the world. So I would seek permission from the chair to allow me to present my ideas.

It is an irony that in a country where the average age of President, Prime Minister, Governors and Chief Ministers are more than 65, very less is being done for the age old people.

Globalization has created disparities between nations and within a nation among states. The natural corollary is migration. The globalization through the electronic media has raised the aspirations of the young people. So, gone are the days when people would be satisfied with their simple living. The communication network has enabled means for migration.

Westernized life style is having its impact in every field of life. The traditional bamboo houses are being replaced by the RCC buildings, the traditional dresses are a thing of past and even indigenous religion Donyi-Polo is giving place to service in churches. But the people who are in their sixties or seventies and who have been left behind by the younger ones are not in a position to change themselves. Their faith in Kebang in Siang valley region or looking for good omen in the liver of a chick in Apatani valley of Arunachal Pradesh is still there. Their myths, their belief cannot be changed so easily.

Globalization, if it has brought affluence, has also created unemployment to a bigger scale. A directionless globalization is no solution to the problems of a semi-primitive society where myths and science go hand in hand. A new model of development must be sought to contain the tide of globalization, which is doing more harm then good for the people of this country.

Following measures are suggested, which may be helpful for the society as a whole.

1. The job opportunity in the rural areas should be explored. For this, stress on indigenous technology should be more than on any imported model. This would help stop migration. The retention of younger generation would help in the caring of age-old people.

2. The villages should be provided with all the modern facilities so that disparity between rural areas and urban areas should be minimum.

3. The health care facilities in the remote areas

should be increased. The major problem with the age-old people in rural areas in Arunachal Pradesh is of health facilities. The model of Uttaranchal of mobile medical van is on the anvil here. In Uttaranchal with the support of TIFAC, (an autonomous council under Department of Science and Technology, Government of India) a mobile medical van was started 4 years back. This van is having a number of facilities like X-ray, ultra sound, ECG etc. The van is covering 4 districts of Uttaranchal. After seeing the success of this mobile medical van, the World Bank has sanctioned one mobile medical van for each district of Uttaranchal. The same experiment is in the process of implementation in Arunachal Pradesh. But seeing the vast area of Arunachal Pradesh, one mobile medical van for each district would be required. So living longer should be accompanied with healthy living.

4. The role of state as welfare state should be enhanced. The protagonist of neo-liberalism, supported by the harbingers of globalization like World Bank and IMF would plead for more and more privatization. But this thesis is adversely affecting already worse position of elders in a developing society. The bare minimum in the form of old-age pensions which is also not available to all eligible should be reviewed and at least an amount which can sustain the livelihood of elders is required.

5. The participation of NGOs and other

organizations dealing with the affairs of elderly should be ensured in every policy decision. Most of the policies of the government bypass this section. The elders are left on their fate.

6. The annual fairs should be organized in every district where the elderly should be given proper place. It will fulfill the cultural aspirations of the elders. The elders are a treasury of oral history, oral literature. Their legacy should be patronized by the state.
7. Academy on Tribal Culture should be founded in the state as soon as possible. It is unfortunate that A.P endowed with such a rich cultural heritage does not have any single academy like state Sangeet Natak academy, Academy on Folk Culture or Lalit Kala Academy.
8. The new structures should be made in the towns which are fully devoted for the elderly people.
9. The institutions of Panchayat Raj should be made effective and these should be equipped with all the modern facilities like computers. It is very shocking to learn that in A.P. where the community feeling is so strong and where community decisions sometimes are binding, the institution of Panchayati Raj in still in nascent stage.

If above suggestions are implemented in right earnest, I hope the position of the elders would improve in this remote state also.

9

Globalization, the Traditional *Arunachalee* Identity and the Psycho-social Gap of the Aged and the Elderly

—*Raju Barthakur*

[The paper is an attempt at giving an overview of certain factors responsible for creating a societal and psychological gap between the aged and the youth in Arunachal Pradesh. The prevalence of linguistic and cultural diversity within a single geo-political entity has imparted a sense of marketability and 'commodified' the Arunachalee culture, to be explored and opened up in an era of globalization. This incursion of the market forces coupled with the rapid advancement in education and other spheres has resulted in the growth of a sub-culture which is a mélange of the old and the new; but in the process, it has alienated a sizeable section of the society comprising senior citizens who are far behind in the pace of socio-cultural growth and are left with nothing but the traditional customs and practices to fall back upon].

Globalization, a term in vogue since 1980s, is

primarily a referent to the process of expansion of economy from a developed to a developing nation and the opening up of the markets of the hitherto insular economies of the world. While the attempt was to create a "global village", or more recently a 'glocal space,' ensuring a 'mainstream presencing' of the 'marginalized' groups, this process in general, has however, has been a subject of vigorous debate as it has created deep schisms within societies over such issues as 'identity' and the emerging psycho-social gap between the aged and the youth. Although the process has resulted in highlighting the relevance of ethnic and cultural identities in the face of global ethnoconvergence, it has, at the same time, resulted making the silence of the 'other' more deafening than ever. As a process, it has placed the concept of identity in a vortex of 'crisis', as Kobena Mercer avers as "something fixed, coherent and stable is displaced by the experience of doubt and uncertainty."[1]

It is against such a backdrop that the triad of globalization, question of tribal identity and the plight of senior citizens has gained prominence world over today. It is more so in India because of a considerable tribal population dotting over central and the North Eastern states.

Arunachal Pradesh alone, for instance, is a home to around twenty three major tribes and 106 sub-tribes along with a host of clans and sub-sub-tribes. Thus, being predominantly tribal, with unique customs and practices followed by the elderly the question of traditional identity and upholding of the indigenous culture has become a real challenge against the s(co)urge of globalization.

Racially, the people of the state are of mongoloid, paleo-mongoloid and proto-mongoloid origins. Dr. Verrier Elwin refers to the people and the societal set up of the erstwhile North East Frontier Agency (NEFA) as the one which "ascends for hundreds of years into the mist of tradition and mythology."[2] The major tribes of the state include the Monpas, Sherdukpens, Hill Miris, Nyishis, Apa Tanis, Adis, Mishmis, Noctes, Singphos, Khamptis, etc. The entire area is marked for its ancient lore and mythological associations preserved and transgenerated orally. The uniqueness of cultural identity owes primarily to the linguistic and cultural diversity that prevail within the geopolitical entity and their harmonious co-existence, which is often perceived to be an "interesting philological puzzle"[3] by the ethnologists and anthropologists alike. This diversity is primarily evident in their costumes, rituals and religious practices, which differ from tribe to tribe even though they reside within the same geographical area. The Monpas of the East and West Kameng districts, for instance, are the believers of the Lamaist Mahayana school of Buddhism. The typical Monpa dress includes a *'chuba'* or 'cloak', usually made of the coarse woolen stuff dyed red. The Monpa man cuts his hair in a straight line just above the eyes and at the level of the nape of his neck behind. Though they come closer to the Monpas in religious and cultural beliefs, yet a Sherdukpen male, on the other hand, is starkly discernible in his cropped hair and the unique skull cap — the *'gurdam'* he uses. Despite being geographically proximate to each other, the Sherdukpen males wear the *'sapo'*, as gainst the *'chuba'* of the Monpas. Speaking of the head gear, the

Nyishis of the Lower Subansiri and the Papum Pare districts wear a wicker work helmet surmounted by the red-dyed beak of the hornbill. It might also have the additional decoration of hornbill feathers. Usually a bun of plaited hair called '*podum*' with a brass skewer horizontally stuck through protrudes on the forehead. Similar examples can be drawn from other tribes inhabiting the landscape of the state, all adding to a single-knit identity of the 'Arunachalee' while maintaining their cultural and traditional individuality.

Such cultural and traditional diversities, combined with their comparative geo-political inaccessibility have rendered a sense of exotic charm to the notion of Arunachal and the *Arunachalee* himself. Historically speaking, the state remained virtually closed to any external influence with almost no appreciable industrial or infrastructural set up. Even now, there is a considerable prevalence of the primitive subsistence economy. This is primarily because of the administrative principles of exclusion adopted by the British government and followed by the succeeding Indian governments. The British rulers in India were sagacious enough to realize the importance of special administrative approach for the areas under the tribal domination in accordance with the spirit of their customs and religion. Thus, they formed these regions into special Non-Regulation Tracts to be administered by simpler codes directly by the Deputy Commissioners. In accordance with the special provision, the Inner Line Regulation was formulated in 1873, thus paving the way for the formation of the Union Territory of Arunachal Pradesh later in 1972, and later on a full-fledged state.

As a result, the state has seen almost no investment in terms of economy. Similarly, the urban centers too are at a premium with most of them are just the administrative head quarters with almost no locational advantage.

With the spread of education amongst the new generation, this sense of isolation has become problematic, and they found it increasingly tough to reconcile to the disadvantages. They started making vociferous demands for development and resented the peripheral treatment towards it by the rulers at the center. This demand for change has created a deep schism within the society as there is a dilemma over the question of preserving indigenous identities on one hand, and embracing change by aligning with the mainstream on the other.

Due to the political, economic and geographical insularity, the advancements in the field of education, science and technology could not percolate to the interior places and as a result, a significant section of population, uninitiated towards these changes were at a loss, and they failed to adapt themselves to the emerging scenario. Consequently, this section of population comprising mainly of the senior citizens were alienated both socially and psychologically, as they could not brace themselves up to the situation. They, on the other hand, cocooned themselves into a shell and clutched on to the traditional values, ethics, customs and rituals.

This sense of alienation is further compounded by

opening the gates of the state to the outsiders. The untrammeled beauty of the state, its exotic charm, its unexplored and pristine natural splendour has succeded in arresting the appeal of the tourists tō explore the unexplored. The exotic insularity has commodified the *Arunachalee* culture and attached a brand name to it. This morphing of cultural convergence posits a potent challenge to the uniqueness of the *Arunachalee* society. A face of systemic incomprehensibility is brazenly apparent in the senior citizens and with this detachment comes, a feeling of creeping social insecurity.

Similarly, their authority over traditional religious belief too, is waning as the new generation is more inclined towards embracing Christianity. The onset of globalization has witnessed a series of attempts at proselytization of the *Arunachalees* thereby putting a question mark on the viability of the indigenous religious practices. The predominant Western view about the religion of the tribal "is more than a mixture of all the various idolatries and superstitions."[4] Further, a conspicuous lack of religious scriptures, regular systems of prayer and permanent places of worship too, is providing a boost to religious conversions. Christianity, propagated as something more organized and secure is weaning away the people from their traditional religious practices. The educational system imparted by the Christian missionaries is also a force to reckon with as the people perceive it to be a gateway to the West. Thus, there is a conscious attempt at the intrinsicalization of the western values and ideas with such missionaries acting as pliant facilitators. These neo-converts, on the other hand, have suddenly become more relaxed and too inhibited towards traditional songs, dances, festivals and rituals. There seems to be a formation of an alternate identity which is marked more for its calculated rejection of the tribal roots and the conscious adoption of a hybridized form of identity. In the process of embracing globalization in Arunachal Pradesh, we find a gradual shift from the clan-based totemistic set up to a translocalized social stratum, a cohesive sphere of ethnic solidarity slowly giving way to heterogenized cultural de-territoriality – a set-up in which the aged and the elderly have become more marginalized, a sizeable section of the "other" whose voice has been muted and subsequently lost in the bustle and din of modernity.

The impact of globalization is often group and region specific. Notwithstanding the fact that it is largely responsible for converging the world into a 'global village' from a macroscopic view point, globalization is also responsible for creating intra-group schisms, especially within such closeted societies as we have in Arunachal Pradesh. Thus, on one hand while we find the educated local inhabitants of the state are apacing themselves with their more advanced counterparts in other parts of the globe, but their educationally challenged, financially strained brethren, and the elderly and the senior citizens who are religiously tied to their generationally beheld traditions, for whom it is too late to embrace the newer challenges and lucrative opportunities, globalization is turning out to be a force that is divisive in nature and in the face of which they are no more than mute spectators. The impersonality of the modern technologies, the market-driven approach, sophistication in style, behaviour and manners is creating a hiatus between the aged and the young which is too wide to bridge. However, one of the possible options to address the problem is to ensure that the changes are proportional to the needs of the society, rather than embracing something blindly and aping others without caring for tradition, cultural values, and above all, a sense of belonging.

NOTES & REFERENCES

1. Bose, M.L.: *History of Arunachal Pradesh.* Delhi: Concept Publishers (1997).
2. Chaudhury, J.N.: *Arunachal Panorama.* Shillong (1973)
3. Elwin, Verrier: '*India's North East in the Nineteenth Century.*' NEFA: Shillong (1955)
4. Elwin, Verrier: '*India's North East in the Nineteenth Century.*' NEFA: Shillong (1955)
5. Elwin, Verrier (1959): *A Philosophy for NEFA.* NEFA: Shillong
6. *Ibid.*
7. Mercer, Kobena (1994): *Welcome to the Jungle.* London: Routledge.
8. Mibang, Tamo (1996): *Relevance of Indigenous Religion. Arunachal University Research Journal,* Vol.1.
9. Riba, Tomo (2003): Tribes in Transition—Advent of a New Religion: A Study on the Impact of Christianity on the Tribes of Arunachal Pradesh. *Arunachal University Research Journal.* Vol.6 (I).
10. Riba, Tomo (1996): Gallongs: Their Belief and Eco-system. *Arunachal University Research Journal.* Vol.1.

10

Welfare Schemes for the Aged: Scenario in Arunachal Pradesh

—*R.P. Bhattacharjee & R.M. Pant*

Introduction

Ageing is a global phenomenon and pinch of this problem is being experienced by all people in all societies. Severity of this global problem was first visualized in the developed countries and now it has become a household concern, including in our country. North Eastern region of India is not immune to this problem and traditional society of Arunachal Pradesh too stands exposed to this problem.

These days there is a lot of talk about the demographic window opened for India by the relatively younger age structure of its population and that is likely to help India in becoming a great power. At the same time, India cannot afford to ignore the fact that its population has been graying at a much faster rate than many industrialized countries. The sheer size of the aged population (85 million), prospects of its phenomenal growth and its socio-economic implications are alarming enough to cause concern to the development planners and policy makers (Kulkarni, 2006). This is equally true for the State of Arunachal Pradesh. There are 29,916 people in the age group of 65 and above and about 20,000 of aged population falls in the range of 60-64 age groups. Thus, 4.5% of total population lies in (60+) age group and 2.7% of total population in the age of 65+. Therefore, proper plans and programmes in this state are the needs of the hour.

Plans and Policies for the Aged in the State

The Government of India announced the new National Policy on Older Persons of India (NPOP) during 1999. The Central Government had already instructed all the States and Union Territories to prepare State Action Plans for the older persons to implement the policy.

In Arunachal Pradesh, there are two types of old age pension schemes implemented by the Department of Social Welfare, Women & Child Development. One is for the old and infirm persons in the age group of 60-65 years, which is funded by the State Government called State Old Age Pension Scheme and another is meant for the person in the age group of 65 years and higher, which is funded by the Central Government, Ministry of Rural Development, called National Old Age Pension Scheme (NOAP). During 2006-2007, 1333 old persons were benefited.

Under State Old Age Pension Scheme, an old and infirm Arunachalees person (male or female) is paid monthly pension of Rs. 150/- for their economic rehabilitation. Under National Old Age Pension Scheme, an old and infirm Arunachalee person of age 65 and above (male and female) is paid monthly pension of Rs.200/-. During 2006-2007, 12923 persons were benefited under this scheme.

Earlier, the pension under this scheme was only Rs.75/- per month. This NOAPS is as per directions issued by Supreme Court of India in W.P. (C) No.196 of 2001 dt.28-11-2001 in Public Interest Litigation titled People Union of Civil Liberties vs. Union of India and Others .The State of Arunachal Pradesh was also one of the respondents. The apex court vide order No.196 dt 03-12-2001, directed that NOAP should be disbursed by 7th of every month to the beneficiaries. The Ministry of Rural Development, GOI makes the allocation in time and it is enforced as per direction of the apex court. It has been estimated that there are14,500 old age persons of 65 and above living below the poverty line and they are entitled to get the NOAP (AOP, 2006-2007:5). The beneficiaries of old age pension in the State during last 5 years are shown in table 1.

Table-1
Old-age pension beneficiaries in Arunachal Pradesh during 10th Plan

(Provisional)

Year Pension	State Old Age	Pension National Old Age
2002-2003	3345	13500
2003-2004	1350	12923
2004-2005	1355	13500
2005-2006	1333	14500
2006-2007	1333*	14500*

*Target.

Sources: 1 Annual Operation Plan, 2006-2007, Social Welfare, Women And Child Development Department, Govt of Arunachal Pradesh, Naharlogun, Pp-22-37

2. Dept. of Planning, *Draft Annual Plan*, 2005-2006 and *2006-2007*.

Here, in this table we find that the National Old Age Pension Scheme is better utilized in the State as compared to the State Old Age Pension Scheme. There are no other plans and programmmes in sight to strengthen welfare base for Old age people in the state.

Conclusion

Arunachal Pradesh is languishing at welfare front for the aged, as virtually no movement for the Old age people is even talked about in the state. The emphasis is mainly in providing pension while there are many other things to be done to improve the socio-economic conditions of the old people. Disbursement of pension is also not free from the charges of corruption as modes of disbursing pension are not very scientifically defined. Besides empowering elders economically, there are many aspects like providing social security and much needed psychological support to the aged people are untouched. Citizens Associations similar to other North Eastern State specially like the Mizoram Senior Citizens Association (MUP) which is affiliated to the Federation of Association of Senior Citizens of India (FASC) can also be encouraged to find long term solution with their active participation. Following recommendations are placed for the improvement in the plight of these senior citizens of the state:

1. It is required to set up State Council for the older persons.
2. It is required to introduce income-generating schemes for the senior citizens.
3. To solve the health problems of the elderly, it is

required to introduce a Geriatric Department or Wards in major hospitals in each districts and free Treatment for the old age population in Government hospitals will go a long way in helping this need special group.

4. Crating platform to utilize the experience of the old people will prove to be of mutual help to both, the state as well as the aged population.

It is very important to open old age homes with the government or NGOs help, considering the widening of gap of old people in villages and the new generation who stays mainly in the town and administrative centres.

REFERENCES

1. Kurkarni,Dr. Sumati (2006): Book Review of "Ageing in India- Socio- Economic and Health Dimensions" by Moneer Alam in *Demography India*, Vol.35,No.1 (January- June, 2006), p. 173.
2. *Annual Operating Plan, 2006-2007*, Social Welfare, Women and Child Development Department, Government of Arunachal Pradesh, Naharlogun.
3. *Draft Annual Plan, 2005-2006 and 2006-2007*, Department of Planning, Govt of Arunachal Pradesh, Itanagar.
4. Lianzela and Vanlalchhawna (2007): *Ageing in North East India (Magnitude of the problem of Elderly Persons in Mizoram)*, Vol.1, pp.107-112, Akansha Publishing House, New Delhi.

11

Participation of Aged Persons in Agriculture: An Overview of Arunachal Pradesh

—G.V. Prasanna Kumar

[The subsistence farming in Arunachal Pradesh necessitates the farmers along with their family members to actively participate in various crop cultivation practices. The migration of rural youth to urban areas as a result of socio-economic growth and development, results in 'geronto farming', in the state. This paper analyzes the agricultural scenario and participation of older people in various agricultural activities of Arunachal Pradesh and proposes few active roles for them to make the agriculture of the state highly productive and environmentally sustainable].

Introduction

Agriculture continues to be an important sector of Indian economy with a 24.8% share in the GDP. Its contribution in terms of providing employment to 235 million people (58.4% of the total rural workforce) has been critical in maintaining livelihoods especially in the rural areas (Registrar General of India, 2001). However, major cause of concern is the increase in the number of aged persons in rural areas (Devi and Bagga, 2006).

Statistics reveals that there are 550 million older people living in the world and 61% of them are hosted by the developing countries. The population of the older people is expected to reach to 1.2 billion by 2025 and 80% of this increase will take place in developing countries (HelpAge International. 2005). The population studies in India reveal that there is going to be a startling change in the shape of population pyramid to the cylindrical chart during the period between 2002 and 2050 as presented in Figure 1 (US Census Bureau, 2002). This shift is owing to the movement of our nation from the status of high fertility and high mortality to low fertility and low mortality. In addition, the life expectancy, which is currently 62.5 years, is predicted to rise to 70.9 years by 2025 (Suttie, 2005).

Need of Participation of Older People in Indian Agriculture

The migration of rural youth to the urban areas as a result of socio-economic growth and development coupled with steady rise in the population of older people has the strong bearing on Indian agriculture. Agriculture in our country has been the preserve of small and marginal farmers (127 million farmers). In terms of number of holdings, the small and marginal holdings (less than 2 ha land) account for 78% of operational holdings and operate about 34.2% of total area (Agricultural Census, 2002). These farmers cultivate their land using their own family labourers basically for self-consumption. As the cost of production using hired agricultural labourers is generally high, working of the farmer himself with his family members is inevitable in these types of farms. Devi and Bagga (2006) reported the "geronto farming", which refers to the farming taken care of largely by older women, in the Meetei community dominated areas of Manipur and Assam.

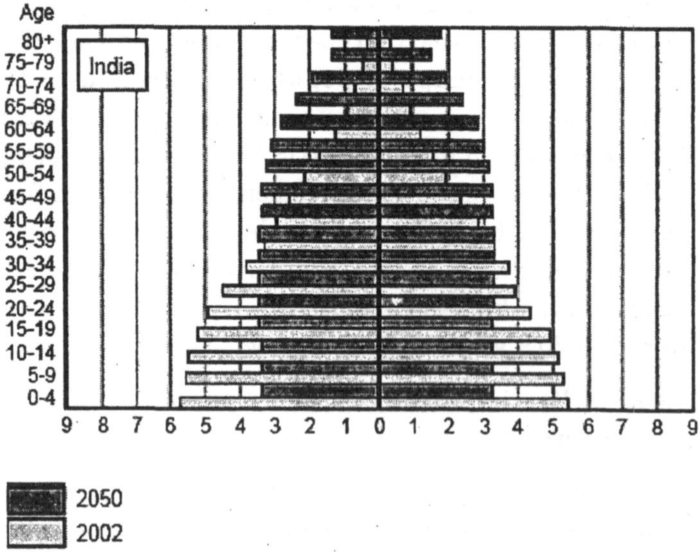

Fig 1. Population pyramid summary for India (US Census Bureau, 2002)

On the other hand, there are about 107.5 million agricultural workers. Judged by the various parameters of quality of life, significant proportion of agricultural labourers lie at the lowest bottom (NIRD, 1999). The average number of days of employment per usually employed agricultural labourer in a year is 333 for male workers and 244 for female workers (NSSO, 2001). Further, there is a high declining trend of employment growth. The average per capita annual earnings of traditional agricultural workers (as of 1998) was reported to be Rs.12300, while it was Rs.14533 for those employed in manufacturing industries. In the plantation sector, the average per capita annual earnings ranged from Rs. 6943 in Tripura to Rs. 24799 in Tamil Nadu (Directorate of Economics and Statistics, 2002). The economic necessity compels the agricultural workers to work as long as they can in farms irrespective of age (Hansen, 1986).

In India, there exists extreme heterogeneity in aged people owing to its vastness and huge population (Ashok and Ali, 2003). Hence, their necessity for involvement in agricultural activities and their vulnerability to various ailments cannot be generalized. This paper makes an attempt to analyze the agricultural scenario and the participation of older people in various agricultural activities of Arunachal Pradesh and proposes few active roles for them to make the agriculture of the state highly productive and environmentally sustainable.

Agricultural Scenario of Arunachal Pradesh and the Participation of the Aged Persons

As Arunachal Pradesh state is characterized by undulating and hilly terrain with wide variations in slopes and altitudes, the farmers practice shifting cultivation in hills and settled cultivation (either valley system or terraced system) in valleys and plain lands.

Shifting cultivation is a unique traditional crop production practice of the north eastern region of India evolved through pressure to generate food under difficult circumstances in hills. In Arunachal Pradesh, this system is practiced to an extent of about 0.11 million hectares (Planning Commission, 2001). As the crop production in shifting cultivation is predominantly subsistence, no agricultural worker other than family members of the household are employed. Though some of the operations like land clearing is done cooperatively by several households together, other cultivation operations are performed by the farmers themselves. In the fields, where settled cultivation is practised, agricultural labourers are largely employed in areas neighboring Assam whereas in the interior parts of the state, farmers themselves are involved in field operations.

It has been found that the farmers in the age group of 40-49 years are more active in agricultural activities in Aruanchal Pradesh (AICRP on ESA, 2006). Further, older people of the household along with their family members participate in many field operations like land clearing, sowing, weeding, harvesting under shifting cultivation and mainly transplanting, weeding and harvesting under settled cultivation. They also participate in post-harvest operations like threshing, cleaning and milling. Most of these operations excluding post-harvest processing are energy intensive (Nag and Nag, 2001).

Old Age and Occupational Hazards in Agriculture

Physiological impairments and other age-related

problems during old age lead to lower work output from the elderly. ICMR (1997) observed that blindness in the older persons in our country is 10 times higher than that prevalent in general population. The hearing impairment in the elderly was found to be 8-9 times higher than that of normal population as a whole (ICMR, 1983). The population of aged with mental morbidity was found to be approximately 1.2 million in 1996 (ICMR, 1987). Prevalence of hypertension was 20 times higher in elderly than the whole population and female were more susceptible to it than male. About 9 million aged people were found to suffer from coronary heart disease in 1996. In addition, the immune system undergoes gradual changes with increasing age rendering the elderly susceptible to a variety of respiratory infections, diabetes, pneumonia and cancers (Ashok and Ali, 2003). In addition, the aged people have slow reflex and it does not allow them to adjust their body to sudden natural occurrences such as sloppy ground, undulating terrain, land slide, rolling boulder, falling tree, presence of poisonous insects etc, which are most common events in the agriculture of the state. Moreover, carelessness increases with increased experience of working in fields (Goodman et al. 1985). The effect of all these factors in the agricultural accidents leading to injuries and permanent disability. AICRP on ESA (2006) reported that about 5% of the total victims of agricultural accidents in the state during the period between 2000 and 2005 were of 60 years or more. Among the aged victims, slow reflexes and carelessness with increased experience were found to be the main causes of the accidents under shifting cultivation.

Rice is the main crop under settled cultivation. The water-rice field is a suitable place for the growth of several types of bacteria, virus, fungi and different parasites. In the developing countries, diseases like malaria, tetanus, hookworm, leptospirosis, schistosomiasis, hay fever, farmer's lung, dermatitis, blepharitis, conjunctivitis and common cold are very common to rice field workers. Joshi (2002) observed the common occupational skin diseases in rice field workers like (1) redness and blisters from prickly rice leaves, (2) abrasions and skin injuries by prickly plants, (3) skin fungal infections (tinea) due to epidermophytes and *monilia* (candida) which may be complicated by secondary sensitization, redness and blisters, frequently due to staphylococcus bacteria, (4) vesicular dermatitis (small blisters) on the feet, (5) itch commonly caused by penetration of the skin by Ancylostoma (hookworms), (6) schistosome dermatitis caused by the penetration of the skin by cercariae, (7) redness, blister and edema resulting from insect stings etc. and (8) calluses of the palms, hands, knees and elbows caused by bad posture and the use of hand tools. Water-rice field is an appropriate field for the breeding of mosquitoes and development of certain parasites such as schistosomes, hookworms, liver flukes etc. People working in such environment are very prone to the mosquito bites and the penetrations into the skin of the certain parasites, which will subsequently lead to certain diseases. A study conducted in Assam has revealed that the afflicted paddy field workers developed exanthema on the exposed parts of their skin mainly legs and arms when they come in contact with water in rice fields (Narain et al., 1994). It also highlighted that rice field dermatitis is an occupational health problem in Assam. Though no epidemiological information on such aspects in Arunachal Pradesh is available, these sicknesses cannot be ruled out as paddy is grown in rainfed low lands and marshy lands in the state. As the older people have lower immunity against these common illnesses, continuous working will bring more harm to them than the quantum of benefit which can be realized from their field work. Further, the ill health accumulated over the life cycle may manifest in old age in an aggravated form making aged people highly vulnerable. Therefore, the following few roles have been suggested for their involvement in sustainable agriculture of the state:

Proposed Role for Aged in the Sustainable Agriculture of Arunachal Pradesh

1. As the physical output from the older people is low, they should be active decision makers for the cropping pattern, crop rotation, variety of seed, water use and conservation, soil regeneration etc. rather than workers in the field. From their long term experience, they can guide their youth better than anybody else.

2. The post-harvest processing operations like traditional threshing, cleaning and drying require comparatively lower energy. The elderly can engage themselves with younger age groups in these activities rather than participating in high energy demanding activities like land clearing etc.

3. Due to increase in population, excessive

dependence on rice and vegetables and pressure to grow the food crops, the shifting cultivation has lost its sustainability leading to the cultivation of few important food crops. Further it has resulted in land degradation, loss of forest cover and increased soil erosion. Otherwise, it involved sustainable production practices of all kinds organic food required for human life in remote hilly areas of the state. The aged farmers of the state have rich knowledge of sustainable practices, which needs to be utilized today.

4. Organic food has the great demand in the world market. The cropping pattern, varieties and crop rotation followed in shifting cultivation is devoid of use of any chemical fertilizers and plant protection chemicals. This is possible in the state in spite of high rainfall and extreme humidity for 8-9 months in the state, which can be adequate condition for fungus and several kinds of insects. The aged can transfer their traditional knowledge in this regard to the younger groups so that scientific background can be given to it for the wide implementation in the region.

5. With aged people in a household, it is easier to add and manage other farm enterprises like poultry, piggery etc. They /can manage the farm workers in absence or busy working days of the younger generation in the household, adding income to the household.

Conclusions

The economic necessity compels the older people of Arunachal Pradesh to actively participate in the various crop cultivation practices. But, the physiological impairments and other age-related problems along with slow reflex and increased carelessness with increase in experience results in injuries and ill health. The injuries and ill health accumulated over the life cycle may manifest in old age in an aggravated form making aged people highly vulnerable. Therefore, attempts must be made to utilize their traditional knowledge on organic food production and give scientific background to it rather than use their muscular energy for various cultivation practices. Thus, the farmers in the old age group in Arunachal Pradesh have a crucial role play in the sustainable organic agriculture and food security.

REFERENCES

Agricultural Census. 2002. Agricultural Census Division, Ministry of Agriculture, Govt. of India.

All India Coordinated Research Project on Ergonomics and Safety in Agriculture (AICRP on ESA). 2006. *Preliminary Report on Agricultural Accidents in Arunachal Pradesh.* NERIST, Nirjuli, Itanagar, Arunachal Pradesh.

Ashok, B.T. and Ali, R. 2003. Ageing research in India. *Experimental Gerontology,* 38 : 597-603.

Devi, D. and Bagga, A. 2006. *Ageing in Women : A Study in North-East India.* Mittal Publications, New Delhi.

Directorate of Economics and Statistics. 2002. Ministry of Agriculture, Govt. of India.

Goodman R.A., Smith, J.D., Sikes, R.K., Rogers, D.L. and Mickey, J.L. 1985. Fatalities associated with farm tractor injuries: an epidemiological study. *Public Health Reports,* 100 (3) : 329-333.

Hansen, R.H. 1986. Major injuries due to agricultural machinery. *Annals of Plastic Surgery*, 17 (11) : 59-64.

Help Age International. 2005. Downloaded from www.helpage.org

Indian Council of Medical Research (ICMR). 1983. *Collaborative study on prevalence and aetiology of hearing impairment.*

Indian Council of Medical Research (ICMR). 1987. *Collaborative study on severe mental morbidity.*

Indian Council of Medical Research (ICMR). 1997. *Collaborative study on blindness* (1971–74). A Report.

Joshi, S.K. 2002. Rice field work and the occupational hazards. *JKMC*, 4 : 11-114.

Nag, P.K. and Nag, A. 2004. Drudgery, accidents and injuries in Indian agriculture. *Industrial Health*, 42 (4) : 149-162.

Narain, K., Mahanta, J., Dutta, R. and Dutta, P. 1994. *Paddy field dermatitis in Assam: a cercarial dermatitis.* J. Communication Diseases, 26 (1) : 26-30.

National Institute of Rural Development (NIRD). 1999. *India Rural Development Report*, Hyderabad.

National Sample Survey Organization (NSSO). 2001. *Employment and Unemployment Situation in India*, 55th Round. Govt. of India.

Planning Commission. 2001. *Report of Working Group on Agricultural Development in Eastern and North Eastern India for the Formulation of Tenth Five Year Plan.* Govt. of India, New Delhi.

Registrar General of India. 2001. *Agriculture Statistics at a Glance.* New Delhi.

Suttie, A. 2005. *Older peoples' services practicing in developing countries.* International Congress Series, 1282 : 448-452.

US Census Bureau. 2002. International Programmes Centre, *International Data Base.*

Index